GOLF

LOWER YOUR SCORE

WITH

MENTAL TRAINING

TOM SAUNDERS MD

Crown House Publishing Limited
www.crownhouse.co.uk

Originally published under the title *Golf: The Mind–Body Connection: How to Lower Your Score With Mental Training* in 1996 by
Mind-Body Golf
105 Sierra Morena Terrace SW
Calgary, Alberta, Canada, T3H 3A2

This edition published by

Crown House Publishing Ltd
Crown Buildings, Bancyfelin, Carmarthen, Wales, SA33 5ND, UK
www.crownhouse.co.uk

and

Crown House Publishing Company LLC
4 Berkeley Street, 1st Floor, Norwalk, CT 06850, USA
www.CHPUS.com

British Library of Cataloguing-in-Publication Data
A catalogue entry for this book is available from the British Library.

International Standard Book Number
1904424538

Library of Congress Control Number
2004111433

Original music: EK Sound
Compact disc recording: Jason Wright, Dark Matter Productions
Editor: Graham Willcocks
Printed and bound in Wales by Gomer Press, Llandysul
Compact disc production: Lemon Media Ltd, Bridgwater, Somerset

In view of the complex nature of individuals, their unique medical or psychological problems and the complexities of the game of golf, this program is not intended to replace professional medical, psychological, or golf advice. The author and publisher expressly disclaim any responsibility for any liability, loss, or risk, personal or otherwise which is incurred as a consequence, directly or indirectly of the use and application of any of this program.

TO MY FAMILY

CONTENTS

List of exercises on accompanying CD

Exercise 1 (Track 2): A Progressive Muscle Relaxation (PMR) exercise for golf

Exercise 2 (Track 3): An exercise to learn self-hypnosis

Exercise 3 (Track 4): A meditation on the focus word Committed

Exercise 4 (Track 5): A meditation on the focus word Confidence

Exercise 5 (Track 6): An exercise to learn to modify blood flow to one's fingers

Exercise 6 (Track 7): A Neuro-Linguistic Programming (NLP) technique, the SWISH, to stop recurring errors in golf

Exercise 7 (Track 8): Explore peak performance feelings (and use them to help develop the feelings in an upcoming game)

ACKNOWLEDGMENTS

This new, completely revised edition of *Golf: The Mind–Body Connection* is now entitled *Golf: Lower Your Score With Mental Training*. It contains new and important information and the exercises are now on one compact disc (CD). The exercises have been edited to be more precise and assume that the reader will learn from listening, practising and using their own words to make the exercises more effective.

I would like to thank the people who gave freely of their time and energy to read the manuscript and offer constructive suggestions for this edition. John Dawson, Tait McPhedran, Don and Carolyn Larsen, Francis Lodato, Elizabeth Van der Wee (she also recorded the introduction on the CD), and Joan Hudson all made very helpful editing suggestions. Bob Pratt, Don Repka, Gayle

Marshall, Al Krebs, Pat Hutchinson, and Barry Flavelle read the manuscript in its early stages and provided encouragement. Carson Manzer made sure that the writing of Appendix A was correct and clearly described his diary concept. Philip Perry, who introduced me to Lars Eric Uneståhl, read the manuscript in its final stage. He offered valuable, constructive ideas, which have been incorporated into the final product.

Thanks to my original editor Tim Cornish for his enthusiasm and for the expertise he brought to the project. Particular thanks go to Cliff Rowell of Hands-On Graphics for his help with the production of the book. Jason Wright of Dark Matter Productions recorded the exercises in his studio with great skill. He was a pleasure to work with.

For this new edition, I would like to acknowledge Dr Donald C. Brown who introduced me to Mark Tracten of Crown House Publishing. Mark's enthusiasm influenced his head office colleagues in Wales to become interested in the program. I have very much enjoyed my contact with Clare Jenkins, Rosalie Williams, Karen Bowman, David Bowman, Tom Fitton and Caroline Lenton. Special thanks to Graham Willcocks whose editorial assistance has been invaluable.

F O R E W O R D

Golf gurus come and go. Yesterday's fad becomes today's trivia. Few if any programs help the golfer achieve the goals these programs set out to achieve. This is not true of *Golf: Lower Your Score With Mental Training*. Dr Saunders' work keeps it simple and helps the golfer understand the methods implicit in mental preparation. His clear, gentle approach to concentration and goal setting demonstrates his years of clinical and golf experience. His successes at improving his own game and at testing and applying these techniques are evident throughout the text.

This work by Dr Tom Saunders is different. It does not promise you the moon, nor does it give you the impression that there is a sleeping giant within that, once awakened, will transform you into a scratch golfer.

It does, on the other hand, offer you sound, scientifically tested ways and means to perform better at golf while enjoying it more. Dr Saunders not only motivates, but also teaches. He does not assume: he explains. He encourages and guides his audience toward improving not only their golf game, but also their personal lives. Furthermore, *Golf: Lower Your Score With Mental Training* provides the means to achieve the goals set forth in the program.

It is difficult to assess adequately how much of any sport is mental. However, regardless of what that percentage is, be it 10% or 50%, the golfer who does not do some properly conceived and scientifically tested mental preparation is not fully prepared to play. This is as true for the professional on tour as it is for the weekend warrior. Dr Saunders patiently and insightfully presents the ways and means by which any golfer may learn mental preparation.

Remember as you read Dr Saunders's program it will not bring your game from 100 to par. Honestly, he doesn't ever pretend to be able to do this. What he attempts to do is to help you concentrate and enjoy the game more, and change frustration to satisfaction.

I have seen this work grow from its earliest stages. The painstaking attention to detail that Dr Saunders has brought to this work makes it a must for anyone who is serious about mental preparation. *Golf: Lower Your Score With Mental Training* will bring a wonderfully practical perspective to your game.

I have introduced Dr Saunders's work to all of my golf clients and friends. I am sure that you will enjoy the program as much as I have.

– Francis J. Lodato PhD ABPP,
Sport Psychologist to the British Columbia Lions
Football Club of the Canadian Football League,
and the Orlando Magic Basketball Organization of the
National Basketball Association

INTRODUCTION

"... this much is certain: golf is a game in which attitude of mind counts for incomparably more than mightiness of muscle."

– Arnold Haultain, 1908

When this program began in 1989 there were few mental training programs available for the average golfer. There were books and videos outlining the psychological aspects of golf, but they didn't really help the golfing reader make that knowledge work for them.

This program combines a source book and a CD. The book outlines the theories and techniques for developing your *inner mental skills,* and the recorded exercises on the CD help you to make that knowledge a part of your mental state for playing better golf.

Golf is essentially about the present moment – now, this shot. You play the shot that faces you, and play it to the best of your ability. And when you are in the middle of one of those flows of good golf, you are not haunted by the memory of bad shots. Your concentration is positive and you don't stand there telling yourself what not to do … how not to play this shot.

When things aren't going so well, however, negative thoughts creep in. Instead of concentrating on what to do, your mental focus shifts to what to avoid – where not to hit the ball, what not to do.

Golf: Lower Your Score With Mental Training explains a quick and effective method for producing more of those great flows of golf, and avoiding the pitfalls and the negative thinking. You will discover how easy it is to develop – and keep – a confident frame of mind for better shot making. You will learn to be positive about your game and to expect to play well. Your enjoyment of the game will increase as your scores improve.

The key lies in the *inner mental skills* that allow you to learn better, to hone your swing, and to increase your enjoyment of the game of golf. Most of our everyday mental activity is logical and sequential. In our normal thinking we spend a lot of time problem solving, analysing and planning. But performing well in sport requires a different sort of thinking. We need to achieve the right level of relaxation, use imagery in creative ways and focus on the here and now, shutting out everything else. These are the *inner mental skills*.

THE PROGRAM'S GOALS

When you have understood the ideas in the book and mastered the exercises on the CD, you will be able to:

- quickly achieve a state of active relaxation – the balanced relaxation that is an integral part of good performance

- use mental imagery to learn and improve your golf game

- develop positive thoughts and behaviour patterns for your golf game

- focus completely on the shot you are about to make

- recall and relive images of your best performances, and project the same feelings into the image of each shot of an upcoming game.

CHAPTER ONE

INNER MENTAL TRAINING

"If my mind can conceive it, and I can believe it,
I then can achieve it."

— *Larry Holmes*

GOLF IS A MIND GAME

Golf can be an exhilarating game when you are playing
well, but it is frustrating and difficult when it is not going
well. When you're playing poorly, with only a few good
shots to relieve the frustration, it's easy to become angry
at yourself, angry at golf. And as well as anger, a range of
other emotions gets in the way of good golf. Those first-
tee jitters when you have to perform in front of other

people, for example. We all get them. They are far more common than you might think.

Or those occasions when you are playing so well that you feel this could be your best score ever … until you start to protect the score instead of playing each shot as well as you can. Then the fear of missing putts takes over, and as you try harder to get rid of the fears the mistakes magnify and those negative emotions get stronger.

It happens because the mind and the body are very closely connected. The way we think of ourselves – our self-image – has a direct effect on our body systems. Our performance suffers when our body systems are not at their best. Overcoming those negative emotions, thoughts and images of you that produce poor perform-ance is one of our key themes.

For tour players and club golfers alike, the difference between winning and losing lies in mental preparation. Jack Nicklaus is quoted as saying that golf is 90% a mental game, although it is difficult to put a percentage on it for the average golfer – the mass of players whose golf skills are not as well grooved as Jack's. Frank Lodato, currently the sport psychologist with the Orlando Magic Basketball team and a successful mental coach, tells his professional players that even if the mental aspect is only 10% of their game, they are not fully prepared to play if they only practise the 90%. They are really ready only when they practice that 10% as well.

The mental aspects of the game are enormously important for learning and improving your golf. So using this program will help you make the mental side of golf work for you, and increase your enjoyment in playing the game well.

SELF-HYPNOSIS

I was reading about the mental training that Olympic athletes go through, and it struck me that there were strong similarities with what I was doing in my medical practice. I was using self-hypnosis to teach my patients how to develop their inner resources, so they could become more self-confident in childbirth, or stronger when facing surgery, chemotherapy or the anxiety of phobias. I used it with some golfers too, to help with specific problems like the putting yips or difficulty sleeping before a tournament.

Rich Boswell, a top amateur golfer, had learned self-hypnosis to help control a medical problem. When I suggested that he could use the same techniques to improve his golf, he created an image of the club-head going through the ball. In that image the club-head would do exactly what he wanted. When he altered his image of what he wanted the ball to do, he did not have to think about changing his stance or grip or even what the club-head should do – all that happened automatically and the shot would draw, fade, go high or low. A great example of the power of imagery in golf. That same year he used the technique and won his place on the Provincial Amateur team. When it rained on the last day of the tournament, he said that his new imagery helped him focus on his shot, not the rain.

Encouraged by this, I asked prominent speakers at conferences on hypnosis whether they had ever used hypnosis techniques for sport. They all had similar stories to mine. Each of them had responded to an athlete's problem as if he or she were a patient. And once the problem was solved, the athletes were encouraged to use self-hypnosis to work on their imagery and concentration skills, for enhanced performance.

From my long medical experience, I knew that the skills and techniques could be taught, and that patients could use the skills without me present. I began giving seminars based on my experience with patients, with very positive feedback from golfers.

And to make sure that there was a solid foundation for my ideas, I carried out before-and-after evaluations using statements about mental skills. When a research psychologist friend analysed the results, he confirmed that they were both significant and positive.

So when I weighed up all the evidence about transferring mental skill techniques from medicine to golf, it was more than enough to trigger this program.

TRAINING YOUR INNER MENTAL SKILLS

High-speed cameras that freeze-frame the tiniest aspects of the golf swing have greatly improved our knowledge of swing mechanics. Techniques like this make teaching and learning the swing much easier – so why hasn't the average golf score come down in line with technological advances, well-groomed courses and the improvements in equipment?

It is because we do not pay enough attention to developing our inner mental skills – because there haven't been the tools and techniques around for us to use. Instead of developing the right mental approach, we over-analyse everything ... and that gets in the way of good shot making.

Any golfer will recognise this situation. You are about to play a shot, and "paralysis by analysis" sets in. With so many things going through your mind – *I have to remember to do that ... I mustn't go over there ... keep that shoulder down* – it's impossible to concentrate on everything at once.

But I know that you can also remember a great shot, when you walked up and hit it with "effortless effort". You were calm yet focused, with a positive blend of concentration, imagination, intuition and "active relaxation".

The idea of active relaxation sounds like a contradiction, but it simply means that there is a balance between your level of relaxation and the level of activation that's essential for good performance. So when we talk about golfers needing to be relaxed, we are not describing the deep level of relaxation used in hypnotherapy techniques, or in stress reduction techniques. You will see a lot more about active relaxation in Chapter Two.

INNER MENTAL TRAINING

Mental training for golf has a tried and tested history. Swedish sport psychologist Dr Lars Eric Uneståhl spent 25 years working with athletes in all sports, developing the idea of self-hypnosis into programs for athletes that he called *inner mental training* (IMT).

He coined the term *inner mental skills* to cover the concentration, relaxation, imagery and intuition needed for performance. These are essential skills because they not only help you play better golf – they're also vital for effective learning. And we can be trained because we have these skills to some extent, and anyone can learn how to develop them.

I have taught IMT principles to everyone from speed skaters to actors … from musicians to patients preparing themselves for surgery. And they were all rewarded with their own benefits – faster times, more confidence, better healing ability. In addition, people who have taken this program tell me of the successful transfer of the skills to their everyday work lives, managing the frustration of difficult meetings or the stress that comes with job interviews. Some have successfully used the skills to help manage medical problems such as back pain, or have coped with stress and anxiety during acute illnesses. Bob Pratt provides a good example in his testimonial.

So anyone can benefit, whatever the level of their inner mental skills at the moment. Most of us are near the average although there are a few exceptional individuals for whom inner mental skills are already an accepted part of their lives and their sport. In the rest of us though, those skills are less well developed – possibly because we do not know much about them, or maybe due to a life-long habit of restricted thinking. Human nature seems to demand proof, right answers and facts … analysing details and distrusting intuition. The education system teaches us to succeed with logic, reasoning and sequential thinking to solve problems. We depend on written words and numbers, conscious effort and deep concentration.

However, analysis and logic are not the most helpful approaches for a better golf swing and consistently lower scores. The key to golfing success lies in the "effortless effort" that is characteristic of inner mental skills.

USING INNER MENTAL SKILLS FOR BETTER GOLF

My own experience proves you can use your inner mental skills to improve your golf.

A few years ago, a reader from Chicago, Bob Husmoller, sent me a brochure on Jack Kuykendall and his Natural Golf Corporation (NGC). Jack had developed a new swing theory and designed clubs to match the swing. He later met Moe Norman, the Canadian golf legend, and Moe's swing matched the principles of the Natural Golf swing.

Moe was the most accurate ball striker in golf and had used his unorthodox swing for fifty years, so the theory and the swing clearly worked. Intrigued with their testimonials and theory, I bought a 6-iron and the teaching video. The accuracy and distance of my shots compared with my traditional swing was amazing, and I switched completely to the NGC clubs and swing. I learned a very different grip, stance and images for the swing. I attended a weekend school and the following year had a few hours of informal instruction from Todd Graves, an NGC teaching professional who was playing the Canadian tour.[1]

This experience gave me an opportunity to put mind–body ideas into practice. I committed myself to use only this new swing for a full season. It was a radical change from the traditional swing I'd used all my life, and from the mental images that went with it. But I taught myself the images necessary for the changes and learned to assess the mental pictures of my swing. When I hit a good shot, I paused to review images of the mental and the physical parts of the swing I was working on.

1. See *Golf Digest*, December 1995, for an article on Moe Norman and a description of Natural Golf's swing theory.

How did I do? Well, my first year's scores were inconsistent, with one or two errors on several holes in most games. Then in the second year, I learnt about the progressive muscle relaxation (PMR) exercise that you'll see in Chapter Two. As I did it regularly and got better at assessing the level of tension in different muscle groups, I realised that whenever I was facing even a moderately difficult shot in a casual game, I started to feel anxious. That made me hunch my shoulders up and hold my breath, as if I were preparing myself to swing hard. The solution to the problem came with PMR, as I focused on the relevant muscle groups and used imagery to create a way to quickly relax them. Still later, I developed my way of using PMR while playing, as you will see.

In my second season with this new swing, I won my division in the club championship and scored two aces, both during tournaments with the second one coming on my last hole, the ninth, during the club championship. My handicap is now lower than when I started the new swing and I have achieved a lifelong goal – a one-over-par game. That was two strokes under my age at that time.

If I can do it you can do it. My experience shows that you will be rewarded with lower scores and more enjoyable golf, when you commit time and effort to this program. And using the skills in everyday living will give you an added bonus.

PMR EXERCISES

In the exercises, I stress that you should use your own words and routine. For example, after I had been doing PMR for some time, I realised that I had missed the group of muscles that turn the torso. So in this edition this move has been added to the PMR exercise. I have also worked in a few exercises that focus on the muscles of the head, neck and the face. A smile is the last direction. It is a great relaxation cue and is cued to the final swing thought that Moe Norman used; he smiled as he wondered how good his shot was going to be! This has served me well, so I believe it is well worth emulating. You may find, as I did, that you will modify your PMR routine to suit your needs and your thoughts about golf.

Now turn on your CD player (or your computer's audio player) to listen to Track 1, the introduction to the exercises. Then do the PMR Exercise 1 on Track 2. I will explain the theory more fully, in the next chapter.

After doing the exercise, write about the experience. A sentence or two in a logbook will record your reaction and ideas for future use. You will notice throughout the book that I have changed triggers, anchors and preshot routines. This is the result of diary keeping, changing as I grow into this new way of playing golf. (See page 99 on writing notes in a diary.)

CHAPTER SUMMARY

Inner mental skills consist of concentration coupled with imagination, intuition and active relaxation. They are the skills that help you perform well, to play the game, and they are part of everyone's makeup. Training improves them just as physical skills improve with training. Think about the application of these ideas to your everyday life.

You will notice that I am focusing on shot making and the mental skills that improve it. That does not mean that there's no need for analytical and logical skills in golf, because there clearly is. For example, you can't play without picking a target, allowing for wind, reading the slope of the green and so on. So once you have built up your inner mental skills, we will look at bringing these two sets of skills together. They operate in the two sides of your brain and in Chapter Five we look at getting the left and right sides to communicate better. For now though, we are working on the generally less well-developed skills. So make a commitment to your-self to learn and practice these skills. The pay-off is great and doing it is enjoyable!

LIFE OUTSIDE GOLF

At this stage, just make sure that you have mastered the exercises. At the end of later chapters, I will suggest a few areas where you can use the skills we have just looked at, to make a difference in your life outside golf.

CHAPTER TWO

RELAXATION FOR PERFORMANCE

ACTIVE RELAXATION

When you are too relaxed, you do not have the drive or the energy to play well. When you're too tense, you try too hard and mistakes follow. This is true in golf more than any other sport.

Most golfers have experienced the exhila-ration of hitting a long

TEE TIPS

Keep your head down
Flex your knees
Firm up your grip
Loosen your grip
Watch the ball
Don't bend your elbow
Step into the ball
Don't rush your swing
Follow through

and

RELAX

– Anonymous, from a poster on a clubhouse washroom wall

ball easily, with no apparent effort. Afterwards, they often remember being relaxed as they made the shot. But when they try hard to repeat that performance, the shot often goes wrong – because they try too hard. Trying hard increases the tension in the opposing muscles, and we need those opposing muscles to be relaxed to the right level, for a smooth and balanced result.

There is reliable scientific evidence to show that in any complicated physical skill, lowering the tension in the opposing muscles improves the performance. Having the right tone in the opposing muscles is the essential component of active relaxation. It is the foundation for all the best performances.

What are opposing muscles?

When we perform an action, there's generally one muscle primarily responsible for the action. For instance, we use our biceps to bend our elbow. There is also a muscle whose main job is to oppose that action ... monitoring the tension and providing a balancing force to create a smooth result. These are the opposing muscles for that action.

So the triceps oppose the biceps when we bend our elbow. And the biceps oppose the triceps when we straighten it again.

Why is this so important?

Leif Janson, the Swedish national archery coach, used accurate sensors to measure muscle tension and activity in archers as they shot. He found that his best archers were expert in relaxing the muscles that opposed those actively involved in shooting.

In champions, these opposing muscles had just the right tone to make the action smooth. And he found the same thing in musicians who played stringed instruments. The best players had the right level of tension in their opposing muscles.

He also worked with a number of tour golfers at the 1994 Swedish Masters, using sensors to measure the opposing muscles in their forearms as each one took ten shots. The information was recorded as tracings, and analysed.

The better players had smooth tracings in each shot, showing that the opposing muscles did their job well, with no wasted effort. There was a remarkably consistent level of tension at the start of each swing and when the ball was struck.

Janson also found that the better golfers were so used to their own technique that they managed their muscles automatically. They didn't know – and couldn't feel – the muscle dynamics of their swing.

The tracings for the less skilled players were much less smooth, right through the swing. This indicated unnecessary muscle action. They were also far less consistent, as the level of tension changed from shot to shot, and at various stages during a swing.

When Janson taught these golfers to relax their muscles, their performance improved.[2]

RELAXATION AND LEARNING

When you are learning any new complex muscle skill, it helps if you first learn how to relax the appropriate muscles. Several studies have shown that most adults carry a level of muscle tension that is higher than ideal for learning a new skill.

It takes at least four weeks for an adult to learn the different feeling of relaxed muscles as against tense ones. And it takes about the same length of time to learn how to control the relaxation level in particular muscle groups. Children can do this more quickly, because they have not yet come up against so many stresses of modern living.

2. Appendix B contains a more detailed description of his study, along with illustrative tracings of the muscle activity in the swings of a touring professional golfer compared with a less skilled golfer.

So, if you are taking lessons from the pro or learning a new technique, practice PMR before heading for the practice tee and keep it going as you work on your swing changes.

PROGRESSIVE MUSCLE RELAXATION (PMR)

PMR is one of the best methods around for learning muscle relaxation. It's a mainstay technique for teaching general relaxation in stress-reduction clinics, where the emphasis is on using mental images to reduce muscular tension. And we know it works because almost 80 years ago, medical studies were showing PMR to be a successful way of lowering high blood pressure from anxiety or habitual tense living.

In relaxation sessions, you'll often hear something like, "Allow the tension to flow out of your body through your finger and toes." And that's interesting because Leif Janson found that the muscles farthest away from a person's centre of gravity give the most information about their general tension level.

Certain muscles are more important than others in a great golf swing. So make sure you include the muscles of the hands, feet and face when you are doing this exercise for golf. For example, pay attention to the muscles of the dominant forearm that you use for the uncocking action in the swing. Focus particularly on the muscles at the top of the forearm, as they are the opposing muscles in this action. Creating the correct level of relaxation in this muscle group is the essence of active relaxation for the golf swing. It will give you a smooth and powerful uncocking action.

In PMR:

- you tighten each major muscle group, then relax and focus on the feeling of relaxation in those muscles for ten seconds or so

- tightening and then relaxing a muscle produces a deeper sense of relaxation in that muscle than if you had simply tried to relax it

- you tighten then relax muscle groups in sequence from toes to head, or head to toes

- after one or two circuits of your body, a sense of overall relaxation develops.

For this program, the most important thing is to learn the feeling of relaxation in the specific muscle groups that you use in the golf swing. I should explain that the only way you could do this scientifically and completely would be to use a biofeedback machine. This would require an expert who would be able to measure the tension in your muscles ahead of time, to know which of your muscles you need to relax, and then to teach you how to relax those muscles during a swing. The advantage of PMR is that it does relax all, or almost all, of your muscles. So you do in fact learn the feeling of relaxed muscles throughout your body, including the important opposing muscles. Leif Janson teaches it as a preliminary to biofeedback training.

There is an added benefit to PMR. An aspiring senior tour player came to me complaining of loss of stamina: after two hours of practise, he would be so tired he was unable to focus, was making errors and practicing those errors instead of improving. He had had an old hockey injury to his right shoulder and this was aggravated by the fatigue as well. The prescription I gave him was to do PMR twice daily until his next visit one month hence. He was highly motivated and faithful to the prescription, even foregoing practice for most of the month. He was more relaxed when I saw him next and was back practicing for a few days before his visit. To my surprise and to his delight, he could practise for four hours every day without fatigue; and his shoulder was much less troublesome.

Each time you finish the exercise, survey your body to check whether any muscle groups are still too tense. If they are, work on some images that will help you to relax them. You may find that experience in other sports helps with the imaging – for example, when I want an image of actively relaxed muscles in my legs and torso, I think of times when I was skiing very well.

At this point, stop and do Exercise 1 again while the ideas are still fresh in your mind.

HOW TO RELAX

Whether you relax by PMR, meditation, yoga or another technique, your mind becomes tranquil and you are less critical of ideas and suggestions. The electrical activity in your brain slows down and moves more to the right side – the half of the brain that's more often involved in imagery.

Herbert Benson, a Harvard University cardiologist, studied transcendental meditation (TM) practitioners. They told him of the relaxed feeling they enjoyed while meditating. Their voluntary muscles relaxed and their blood pressure dropped. Their metabolism, breathing, heart rate and brain activity all slowed down. He called this the *relaxation response* and developed the theory that this is a natural physiological response, the opposite of the fight-or-flight response. (See page 88 for a description of fight-or-flight.)

Benson also examined other methods of developing a relaxed state and found that they shared a series of common characteristics:

- sit comfortably

- close your eyes to help empty your mind

- allow your muscles to relax

- breathe in quietly through your nose

- allow the breath to go without force by relaxing your chest muscles

- repeat a humming word such as "one" or "om" on breathing out

- give yourself a definite time for the exercise, for instance, ten minutes (TM practitioners say twenty minutes).

The point is that when you experience the relaxation response, your muscles are not all completely relaxed, as they are in deep sleep. In hypnosis or meditation you are usually sitting, so the muscles required to maintain this posture are working at the correct level of tension. However, the overall feeling is one of relaxation, and it is this feeling that you will have after the PMR exercise.

COMBINING IMAGERY AND RELAXATION

It is hard to relax by telling yourself to do so – and the harder you try the harder it gets. An easier way is through imagery. We look at this in detail in the next chapter, but try this exercise for now – it shows the power of relaxation and imagery:

> Choose a partner of about equal strength and height, and face one another.

Partner One: Place your hands, palms up, on your partner's shoulders. Straighten your arms and consciously tense all your arm muscles to the maximum, even making fists to accentuate the stiffness. Tell your partner when you are ready.

Partner Two: Try to bend Partner One's arms at the elbow using a steady force. Do not jerk suddenly as you may injure them.

Both of you: Judge how much force it takes to bend your partner's arms, or to keep your arms straight.

Then repeat the test, with the following changes:

Partner One: Again, place your hands, palms up, on your partner's shoulders. Take a few moments to relax your arms and hands, and then form an image of unbendable steel bars running through your arms from your shoulders, through your fingers and beyond. When you have this mental image firmly established, tell your partner you're ready.

Partner Two: Again, try to bend Partner One's arms at the elbow with a steady force.

Then switch roles, repeat the process and compare notes on the force needed this time.

You may both be surprised at how much easier it is for Partner One to keep their arms straight the second time around, by combining imagery with relaxation.

Bringing it together for golf

Active relaxation – the balance of relaxation versus activation – is the goal of all athletic performance. It is just as important for the beginner as for the competent golfer.

Build the active relaxation of important muscle groups using the PMR exercise. Only the muscles needed for the shot need to be active – the opposing muscles will have just enough activity to make the movement smooth. All other muscles will have only the tone needed for a relaxed, comfortable, athletic posture. And of course there must be a certain amount of activation, of competitiveness, of wanting to make a good shot.

This image of active relaxation will help you perform to your maximum efficiency, whether for a delicate chip shot or a long tee shot. And as you develop your imagery for golf, focus on the *feeling* images that relate to your sense of position, movement and muscle tension.

CHAPTER SUMMARY

A golfer who is too tense will play badly. A golfer who is too relaxed will also play badly. Golfers must know the feeling of a correct balance between the activation needed to play and the relaxation necessary to perform well. The aim is to achieve this active relaxation, to recognise when you are in this state, and to know how to fine-tune the state.

Why not promise yourself to practice PMR for golf, every day for a month? It will only take fifteen minutes out of your day and you can do it just before sleep. You will become increasingly aware of the feeling of relaxation in your main muscle groups and it will help you to image the correct level of active relaxation in those muscles important in the golf swing, especially the ones that give your swing its smoothness.

LIFE OUTSIDE GOLF

The next time you're facing a stressful event like a presentation to a group, or a job interview, assess the tone of your neck, chest and shoulder muscles. Do it before and afterwards. Then prepare yourself for similar events in future by practicing PMR, paying particular attention to those muscles.

CHAPTER THREE
CREATING IMAGERY FOR GOLF

"The world should o' followed the lead of
pith-uh-gor'-us." He almost whispered the words.
"And 'tis this—to ken the world from the inside,
not the outside as we've done.
Like I showed ye wi' yer gowf shots there."
— Shivas Irons in Michael Murphy's
Golf in the Kingdom *(1972)*

CREATIVE DAYDREAMING

When we daydream, the right half of our brain – the creative imaging side – is active. Our usually dominant left brain – the logical analytical side – goes quiet. It's the same thing that happens in hypnosis, yoga, Zen, meditation, deep relaxation and biofeedback.

We tend to create images in just one of our senses – seeing, hearing, feeling or, rarely, smell – as we narrow our awareness to our "favourite" sense. There's usually a calmness of mind, a feeling of relaxation and a sense of detachment from our surroundings. We drift away and virtually lose ourselves in an image that our brain is creating.

Watching a tournament on TV in 1967, I was startled by one scene. As a player was going through his pre-putting routine, it began to rain heavily. By the time the ball rolled into the hole there was a lot of water on the green. To watch him, though, it was as if the sun were shining. He seemed completely oblivious to any discomfort.

His behaviour reminded me of patients I had taught to use self-hypnosis, who learned to be so involved in an image that they seemed unaware of discomfort. I became intrigued and began to think of ways to try to duplicate that level of concentration in golf.

I noticed that when I putted well, I had a five-part-routine that seemed to make the stroke automatic. So I organized my putting to make sure I always went through all five points. Now when I walk on to the green, I check the slope and contour, the firmness of the ground, the grain and the length of the grass and the length of the putt. Finally, I choose the line and weight.

Then I place all that information into my mind and trust that it will come out correctly. I focus on the imaginary line the putter must pass over as it goes through the ball. And I use a simple hypnosis trick – I breathe in as the putter goes back and breathe out as I stroke the putt. This triggers an automatic and trusted stroke.

CREATIVE IMAGES

In the 1947 movie, *The Secret Life of Walter Mitty*, Danny Kaye played a timid bank clerk. One minute he was a meek clerk, the next he was a famous Spitfire ace in the middle of an air battle. To Walter, everyday life and his dream life were equally real. He had a vivid imagination and fabulous daydreams.

Daydreaming is an altered state. So is self-hypnosis, but it's one where we exercise control over our images. In self-hypnosis we direct our daydreams using suggestions that create images. So when you or I create our own golf images, they will be much closer to reality than Walter Mitty's daydreaming fantasies.

Exercise 2 is an imaging exercise that begins with a shortened PMR routine. Then I describe a garden scene, to teach you how to create a relaxing image. In the scene, I suggest images in each of your senses – sight, hearing, movement and the sense of smell – to maintain and deepen the altered state. The images in one of your senses will be sharper and easier to achieve – which is normal as we all have a favourite sense system. However, another sense system does sometimes seem to take over as favourite for the day, so it pays to practice with all the senses when creating images for golf.

For instance, if the negative visual image of a shot going astray interferes with the positive image of a ball flying to the target, focus on images with your other senses. Create an image of the feel of the swing, or the sound of the ball being hit on the sweet spot as it meets the club perfectly. Before long the first visual image recedes into the background as you make the shot.

IMAGINE YOU CAN DO WHAT YOU'VE NEVER DONE BEFORE

When you face a shot you've never played before, or you are in the sort of place you have not had to play from, use imagery in more than one sense system. Create the best possible shot in your mind, and then focus on this image as you make the shot. You will find that the image becomes reality. The shot you play is no longer unknown … you saw it and played it as an image.

IMAGES ARE REALITY

Creative imagery helps break negative patterns, create a positive reality and overcome the negative emotions that arrive with many images, in the real world. For example, if you are angry with yourself after a bad shot, that anger is the dominant emotion governing your next shot. It attaches itself to the image of the shot you're about to make and leads you to unconsciously expect a bad shot.

And haven't we all told ourselves, "I had better not hit out of bounds," and done exactly that? The phrase "I had better not" isn't an image. It's just words … a wish. The image in our mind is the ball going out of bounds – and that image wins out every time when we face a choice between what we would like to happen and what we imagine actually happening.

Another way of thinking about this is to see images as reality. As we create the image of going out of bounds, we are mentally practising that shot, rather than the shot you really want to make. One experimenter attached sensors to the muscles of a skier, who then used his self-hypnotic state to recall the image of racing down a specific course. The tracings showed that his muscles were active, and the detailed muscle activity actually followed the course of the race course on that hill. As far as the athlete was concerned, he was racing.

SUGGESTION AND IMAGERY

Once you focus on an image in any of the sense systems, it is very easy to slip into a dreamlike state. When you're that relaxed you are much more ready than usual to accept suggestions (from outside, and your own self-suggestions). This is particularly true if those suggestions are phrased in a way that evokes images. Perhaps this is because our memories are often in images rather than in words. They appear complete, with feelings attached, like dreams.

The suggestions in the recorded exercises use words that evoke images – an important factor when you are creating suggestions for yourself. For example, when you want to create suggestions that emphasize control of body systems, you are working on one aspect of control, that of blood flow to that system. Our body uses blood flow to increase or decrease the activity of that system and it does so by modifying the activity of the smooth muscles which make up the walls of the blood vessels. These muscles contract and relax at a rhythm of their own, unlike the voluntary muscles. Just like muscles you can control, these involuntary muscles also need the right tone to be at maximum efficiency for their work.

When you have learned to relax the muscles that make up the walls of blood vessels and the heart, you can modify your heart rate. You can learn to decrease digestive symptoms associated with high levels of anxiety. And as you learn to control some of the symptoms of anxiety, you find that it gets easier to manage the anxiety itself.

Suggestion in self-hypnosis

Suggestion is the factor that makes hypnosis different

from other disciplines. One of the first suggestions you hear as you are led through the hypnosis experience is that your muscles will relax. This is why the PMR exercise is often used to begin a hypnotherapy session, particularly with very anxious patients.

Relaxation is then linked to breathing. As you breathe out quietly without force, your diaphragm and chest-wall muscles are relaxed as your elastic lungs push the air out. As you focus on one sensation – in this case relaxing your breathing – it is easier to develop a tranquil mind and slip into an absorbed, dream-like state.

To the observer, someone in hypnosis may appear to be dozing. However, even though their eyes are closed and they seem unaware of their surroundings, the brain activity is still that of an awake and active brain.

For the person experiencing the altered state of hypnosis, it is the opposite of sleep. They are actively focused on the image, thought, activity or sensation they're involved with. They are aware of their surroundings, but detached from them unless they have a bearing on her task. For instance, a woman using self-hypnosis during childbirth is clearly not asleep. And an athlete who plays on with an injury that would normally immobilize her may be so focused on the game that she is almost oblivious to the pain.

Self-hypnosis is easier for some people than others. Anyone who has already discovered self-hypnosis will have little or no difficulty focusing, relaxing and creating images for their sporting performance. Most of us, though, have to work at learning the skills, as we have to learn the golf swing. But it really is worth the effort. Not only do these skills improve our golf, they are also useful in everyday life.

This exercise (2) is a model for self-hypnosis. Initially, I act as your hypnotist, guiding and teaching as I lead you through the experience. Over time you will start to lead yourself through it, until it becomes easy. I recently asked a patient about a cassette tape I made for her in my office.

She said she no longer used it because she knew the routine by heart and now used her own words instead of mine.

UNPACKING THREE KEY IDEAS

There are three ideas in this exercise that need a little explanation.

1. Anchoring

This is a simple idea that works at the unconscious level, although it can also be a conscious act. An anchor is something in one of the senses – a movement, touch, a sound you have heard or something you've seen – that brings back feelings you associate with the memory. For instance, a particular song makes you cry or smile because the sensual experience carries certain personal memories. Or someone with a fear of flying gets frightened at just the sight of an aeroplane, or the sound of an aircraft engine.

I developed an anchor to use when I get tense playing golf. In my own full PMR routine, I break the process up into the body sections, so when I reach my buttocks in the lower limb section, I pause and say to myself, "One, two, three, relax" three times. At the same time, I focus on what it feels like to have actively relaxed legs. I do the same when I reach "hunching then relaxing my shoulders", and focus on what my torso feels like when it is actively relaxed, and again for my upper limbs, then my head and face.

It works well but it is a bit too long to use as you prepare to take a golf shot. So I have developed a shortened version that is now my set of anchors in my preshot routine. "One, relax" is for my legs, "two, relax" for my torso, "three, relax" for my upper limbs and "four relax" for my neck and face muscles. Doing this as I approach the shot or as I set up to the ball, gives me an anchor set that lets me experience the active relaxation I need, just before I make the shot.

I've also created a trigger for the actual shot. I smile to myself and wonder how good the shot is going to be. It rewards me with more consistent shot making and it could well do the same for you. It takes a little practice, but you may like to try it once you've mastered the following methods that use more simple hypnotic suggestions.

2. Inner strength, or inner coach

There is a part of us that knows our strengths. It has seen us through many difficulties in the past. Think of it as a coach, helping us to develop our natural abilities.

Daydreaming is great, but it can be unrealistic. Your inner coach is there to inject a dose of reality into your daydreams, to tell you whether your golf imagery is nearer to reality than fantasy.

Being able to talk to and trust this inner voice can be extremely useful in handling golf problems. Johnny Miller put a lot of his success in the 1970s down to listening to the "little voice that talks to me" (*Golf Illustrated*, October 1990).

3. An inner mental room

In your imagination, you create a room where you keep specific items that you use in the exercises. This room becomes your own private mental practice area.

It's somewhere where you can focus your mental exercises for golf. For example, in the problem-solving exercises, you create scenes and graphics on the imaginary television monitor in this room. The image of being in your inner mental room also shows that you are deeply enough into your altered state for the exercises to be effective.

Now – with these important concepts still fresh in your mind – this is a good place to put down the book and listen and do Exercise 2.

RELAXATION AND IMAGERY WHEN YOU PLAY GOLF

Let's look a little more at creative imagery. You have worked on the exercises for relaxation and imagery, so we now need to combine them for practical use on the course.

You can bring them together quickly and unobtrusively as you walk up to your ball just before you make your shot. Try them out first on the practice tee. You'll find that as your imagery improves, you become more focused on the shot.

1. Decide on a trigger to start the automatic concentration process. My trigger is the first step I take as I approach the ball.

2. As you stand behind the ball looking at your target, develop the image of a wave of active relaxation … starting at the top of your head and flowing down your face, neck, shoulders, chest, and into your arms and hands and on down.

3. Move up to the ball, take your stance and make the shot while the feeling is still with you.

Another way is to create an image of yourself, as you imagine yourself playing with the ideal level of active relaxation. This is a feeling image and it could come from a memory of a best performance, a great shot or maybe even a shot from a practice session. Once you have the image, move yourself into it and become one with the image.

The great thing is that your imagination is limitless. You can create any image you like, and sometimes the off-the-wall ones work best. For instance, I have a friend who imagines a large magnet drawing him into the image of a great shot he played. It works for him.

CHAPTER SUMMARY

Mental images are reality to our mind and body. When we have an image in our mind of the shot we are about to make, the neuromuscular pathways are active for that shot. It is as if we had practiced the shot just before actually making it. Make a commitment to using imagery to enhance learning and to groove your golf swing. Learn to focus on the image of what you wish to achieve, the ball landing on the target, and remember to practice imagery in all your sense systems, feeling the swing you are about to make or hearing the ball hit the sweet spot.

LIFE OUTSIDE GOLF

Imagine yourself having a very successful interview. Practice this imaging during the few days before the scheduled interview and while waiting to be called into the interview room.

CHAPTER FOUR

KEEPING YOUR EYE ON THE BALL

"The ability to control thought processes, to concentrate on a task (e.g. to 'keep your eye on the ball') is almost universally recognised as the most important key to effective performance in sport."
— *Robert M. Nideffer*

CONCENTRATION

Concentration in golf involves a focus on a narrow, restricted area of attention.

When you resolutely direct your attention toward one activity, several things happen. One is that you reduce or block out other sensations, whether the activity you're concentrating on is real activity or imaginary. Also, narrowing your attention to a very few things is a way into the altered state of awareness – the hypnotic or meditative state that is like daydreaming. And it is an example of the effortless flowing concentration you need for good shot making.

Concentration is one of those things that gets worse as you try harder. You cannot force yourself to concentrate. It has to be effortless and you must allow yourself to be absorbed in the shot facing you. As you are about to make a shot, suddenly thinking, "I must concentrate" is likely to have exactly the opposite effect.

Golfers who look completely absorbed in a shot are creating images, relaxing, going through an anchoring routine and preparing themselves mentally. They are not concentrating on concentrating.

Jack Nicklaus looks as if he's in a world of his own during every shot. When playing in England he was lining up a putt when a large jet flew over, quite low and very noisily. When someone asked him whether the plane had put him off, Jack said, "What plane"?

He maintains that playing the ball to a target in a certain way depends 10% on his swing, 40% on his setup and stance, and 50% on his mental picture.

To achieve concentration, he takes time to become absorbed in his imagery. He says, "First I see the ball land in the target area, then the flight of the ball to that target, and finally, I focus on the feeling of the swing for that shot." Remember that images are reality, so Jack's method is like practicing the shot just before he makes it. Like the skier I described in Chapter Three, his muscles are busy with the image of the swing just before he makes the shot.

A GREAT PRACTICE ROUTINE

The next time you practice, stand behind the ball and pick a target within reach of an easy short iron. Take a moment or two to imagine the ideal flight of the ball to the landing target and then see it rolling up to the actual target.

As you move up to the ball and take your stance, imagine the feel of the swing for that shot. Make the shot with only this image in your mind.

Develop the habit of stopping for a moment or two after each shot to reassess the imagery. You might find a key part of the imagery that can become the trigger move to make the shot happen automatically.

You can extend this type of imagery practice by imagining hitting different shots ... playing out of trees, under a branch of a fairway tree or over a bunker. Then when you have to play these shots in a game, you will find yourself thinking positively and much better able to focus on what you want to achieve.

This sort of practice improves your imaging capability and your concentration, for any shot you might face. At the same time, you learn to depend less on your analytical "what if" thinking and more on the images of the shot you are about to make.

Practice this kind of imaging at quiet times in your day, when you take a few moments' break from work. And if you include conditions of actual play in your images, you will become better able to deal with the distractions and disturbances of real everyday play.

MORE ON ANCHORS AND ANCHORING

One of the most frustrating things about golf can be when you try to transfer those brilliant practice-range shots to the golf course. Something happens that changes what we did on the practice ground and makes us do it differently when we are playing for real.

There are many excellent books and articles outlining good practice routines. One thing they all have in common is that they tend to stress two things. One – be wary of just hitting one ball after another and two – practice with a purpose in mind.

I would add a third. Practice your inner mental game each time you are on the practice fairway or green, even for your warm-up session before a game. Make sure you repeat your pre-shot routine at least every third shot or so, even if it is only in your mind because the practice ground is crowded or there are other physical limitations. Then pause to review the image of good shots, perhaps even closing your eyes as you do – especially if you are working on one aspect of the swing.

I also suggest that you can use the anchoring technique to transfer your practice ground success to the course. We looked at anchoring in Exercise 2, where movement and touch were associated with the feelings of confidence, relaxation and control in the image that you were involved with. So when good shots follow one another in practice, create an anchor to fix the feelings of confidence, active relaxation and self-belief that are essential for great shot making. Spend time focusing on the tempo of your good shots and create an anchor for this feeling. For my friend Rich, the feel of his favourite club is his anchor, so he takes it out and swings it through the long grass beside the tee to reinforce or regain his feel for his best tempo.

Remember your other sense systems as well. Pay attention to the sound of the club striking the ball on the sweet spot … and look for a visual anchor, such as the position of the clubhead behind the ball.

The great thing about anchors is that they work for you automatically. Although the anchor itself is a conscious act, you do not have to think about what the anchor will do.

AN EXAMPLE OF AN ANCHOR

One way to create an anchor is to recall an image of a time when you played a particular part of your game very well. I used this method with Darryl James during a tournament, after he told me that he'd developed a fear of sand shots. He said he was lucky to be leading the tournament with one round to go, even though I had seen him make a great shot out of a fairway bunker to within five feet of the pin.

After his round, we went to the practice bunker. I asked him to close his eyes for a moment and to search his memory bank for a time when he felt completely confident playing these shots. He easily remembered that when he was a teenager he was making – and winning – small bets on holing out from the sand. With this imagery in his mind, he began to hit excellent shots.

Then I asked him to find one particular thing in one of his sense systems that he was doing every time. He then played several shots with that single image in mind. We'd then take a short break and change to the next sense system. I think we started with sight and moved on to feeling. He was able to find one constant image in each system, but the most powerful was the way he placed his right hand on the club just so, as his last move before making the shot. He continued to practice this anchor

until he was 100% sure it worked. And he carried on practising it in his imagination when he was not playing.

On the seventeenth hole of the last round, he hit his
tee shot into a trap. He now faced a fifty-foot shot to a pin
set close to the far side of the green, with a sharp drop-off
into a large pond. He made a magnificent shot to about
three feet, sank the putt and went on to win the
Provincial Amateur title by one stroke.

AN ANCHORING EXERCISE

We all have days when every chip is good, so we'll use
chipping as our example. Imagine that your short game is
going so badly that you now get anxious when you face
any chip.

This is how you structure a practice chipping session:

- Spend a few moments getting the memory of good
  chips into your mind. Take the time to fill in as
  much detail as possible.

- Fix the image by anchoring it in one of the senses – perhaps hearing the clubhead hit the ball or looking at a spot on the ball. Or maybe placing a finger a certain way on the grip. It could be anything that works for you – your imagination is the only limiting factor. Incidentally, please do take some time with this part of the exercise.

- Practice using that anchor until you are completely happy that it's fixed in your subconscious. This will then become the anchor you use when you feel anxiety rising.

- Practice the anchor in your image mode at quiet times in your day. (To find out about your best "take-a-break" periods, have a look at *Ultradian rhythms* in Appendix B.)

These problem-solving techniques can be extremely useful, even though the simulated problems are not the most pressing problems for you. I have included a more complex problem-solving technique called the Swish.

This is best for recurring problems such as those outlined in Exercise 6. It was designed for curing phobias and, in many ways, the problem situation used in the simulation is reminiscent of a mild phobia.

TRIGGERS

Like anchors, triggers work at the unconscious level. But while an anchor is a conscious act, a trigger helps make an action an automatic event. You use an anchor when negative feelings are interfering with your play and a trigger every time, for consistency.

In golf more than any other sport, perhaps, a consistent approach to each shot is essential for success. Repetition increases concentration and this is why pre-shot routines are so effective an aid for concentration.

Use the same movements in the same order to move yourself into a focused mode. That helps make your shot making a smooth automatic event. A *trigger* is when we use a certain action to begin an automatic activity. We start most of the intricate everyday activities that we now do easily, with a movement or action that moves us into automatic mode. It's a mental shortcut that saves your brain having to think about every step of the action, every single time. With repetition, a trigger becomes a useful tool to make shot-making an automatic process. It should be the first action in your pre-shot routine.

When tour player Lee Janzen aims along his club at the target as he begins his final walk to address the ball, it's a dramatic example of a trigger in golf.

Develop triggers to begin moving yourself into the automatic mode of shot making, where everything happens smoothly. Make the trigger an action like Lee Janzen's, or the time-honoured forward press, to make your swing an automatic experience. The best triggers are ones you design for yourself on the practice tee.

KEEPING YOUR EYE ON THE BALL

BEATING NEGATIVE TRIGGERS

Sometimes, a movement that is part of a routine can become fixed in your unconscious as a negative trigger. If you have developed a change for the worse in your shot making, try this technique. It isn't as complicated as it sounds and when you are in your image mode, it is quick and simple.

- Use self-hypnosis to review your pre-shot routine in detail.

- Use the TV in your mental room to watch yourself perform.

- Allow yourself to become involved in details to deepen your altered state and to search for a new move that has crept into your swing.

- Place this move in your memory bank and then recall a time when you were making good shots consistently and review these shots in detail.

- Compare the two swings and check whether a different move has become a negative trigger and is the reason for the change.

Some time ago, I reviewed my routine to find out why there was such a difference between practice and play in my game. In practice, I made shots with a smooth transition to the downswing, but during a game there wasn't this same smoothness. I would grab the club at the top of my backswing, tense the muscles of my upper body and grunt. But then I learnt that I could not grunt if I had no air in my chest ... and if I didn't grunt, I was more likely to stay relaxed through this part of my swing.

I challenged the habit by picking up a trick from baseball pitchers. Several of them start with a deep breath, and then they blow all the air out just before they throw the ball. So the last conscious act in my pre-shot routine is a smaller breath out, just before the club goes back. It does help me make a smoother swing.

CHAPTER SUMMARY

Concentration is essential for good shot making. Anchors and triggers are practical strategies for improving concentration on the shot you're about to make. They are easily learned. Develop a trigger to start your pre-shot routine and move your shot making into automatic mode. Find and practice anchors that will override negative feelings when you're faced with this shot in tense situations. Then allow yourself to become involved with the images of what you wish to accomplish.

LIFE OUTSIDE GOLF

Anchors are also effective for life outside golf. They can help you improve performance at work and in social situations.

CHAPTER FIVE

PLAYING GOLF WITH A POSITIVE MENTAL ATTITUDE

"A bad shot was never on my mind. Every time I got over the ball I wondered how good the shot was going to be. I knew it was going to be good. But how good?"
– Moe Norman (from Lorne Rubenstein,
"Moe's Musings", in Senior Golfer)

NEGATIVE THOUGHTS FOR NEGATIVE RESULTS

You regularly hear golfers say, "I can't putt to save my life," or make some other negative comment about their game. It's as if golf is a victim culture where we feel that it's all down to the forces of darkness. Even tour players act as if the golf gods have something personal against them, as they rage at the result of their shot. Playing the victim can be a dangerous mindset because it fosters the "poor me" attitude – and that leads to, "Bad things always happen to me; I have no control over this, so I'll never improve my game."

Maybe it's because we often say things in a negative way in our society, to reinforce a point. Ask a planeload of tourists what their foreign holiday was like and they invariably give you the bad news first. No mention of the great weather or the excellent food … just the insects and the noise from a nearby building site. So perhaps we are used to accepting negative suggestions too easily.

On the golf course these negative emotions tend to simmer for several holes. And while they do they over-power the positive images that could get you back on track. Far too many golfers miss a putt and then play the next three holes badly, because they're reliving that putt and not facing the opportunities of the shot they're playing now.

It would be a positive move to accept the result of a bad shot and welcome the challenge it adds to the next shot, perhaps even the creativity needed to make that shot. But we can't really control our emotions so it's impossible to turn negative emotions into positive ones at will. We can temporarily drive them out by thinking of something else, but they lurk in our subconscious, ready to pop up again at exactly the wrong time.

The real problem with this negative self-talk – becoming angry with yourself or putting yourself down – is that it increases the likelihood that the bad play will repeat itself. Negative self-talk becomes a negative affirmation and a self-fulfilling prophecy. You expect the bad shot to happen again – and soon. And it does.

DEALING WITH STRONG NEGATIVE MEMORIES

Strong negative memories form when we go through severe emotional and/or physical stress. They not only have powerful emotions attached to them, they also have a chemical impact. During a stressful event, hormones and other messenger molecules flood the body and produce a rapid pulse, trembling hands, dry mouth, a tight feeling in the stomach and so on. Performance suffers.

Large amounts of these molecules lie there quietly in the organs that produced them, ready for immediate use if a similar event occurs. So when we remember an event, we also recall and experience the associated feelings, because the hormones and other messenger molecules are triggered by that memory, or by a similar experience. Even the memory of that event will trigger their release.

So our own bodies work against us at times by producing an *anxiety response*. And it gets worse over time rather than better, as our organs store a lot of spare chemicals. Someone has an anxiety response to teeing off in front of the whole club in a match. But the next time they have to play a shot in front of just a few strangers, the feelings are even worse, out of all proportion to the severity of the situation.

The question is – how can you manage situations that trigger an anxiety response?

- Start by seeing the signal for what it is – a negative suggestion that triggers the same feelings in any similar situation.

- Then, make up an alternate positive thought or affirmation. Phrase it in the present tense, not the future – so *I am* rather than *I will*. And positive … *I am (calm)* instead of *I am not (anxious)*.

- In the meditative state, create a positive image of the behaviour change you have in mind.

- Make up an affirmation, a word or phrase that evokes the image of achieving that behaviour change. Repeat the affirmation often, quietly and firmly, like a whisper in your mind to reinforce your subconscious image.

Over time the negative thought or suggestion will gradually lose its force, or disappear. The affirmation, the image of the changed behaviour will replace it and become a part of the way you view yourself as a golfer – your self-image.

AFFIRMATIONS FOR GOLF

Throughout this program, I suggest that you practice the altered mode of control, the meditative state, as it's the most efficient way to achieve behaviour change. When your brain is quiet, it approaches problems in a more intuitive, holistic, right-brain way. The usually dominant and analytical left side of your brain is in the background. And as images are powerful, when you are relaxed and you use an affirmation – a word or phrase that evokes the image of achieving a change in behaviour you want to make – that image is powerful enough to control the shot you are about to make.

Meditation exercises on the CD describe the images I use when I want to be positive in golf. I have chosen affirmations on two C-words that evoke images that help me to fix my thoughts on any golf shot: I am COMMITTED, I am CONFIDENT.

For me, each word and the image it evokes are important. They help me become and remain focused on any golf shot. The ideas and images that these words represent to me are woven into meditations in Exercises 3 and 4. The meditations are my thoughts and are meant to be models around which you can build your own meditations.

Creativity is another useful C-word. Darryl James, a former top amateur golfer and Canadian tour player, plays better when there's a friendly encouraging crowd following him. So he creates the image of a crowd encouraging him in tournaments. Images like these are easy to use, and since they are unique to you, are very effective. Amy Alcott, the LPGA tour player, says that she thinks of each of her shots as a new creation. In every round, we may face one or two shots we have never had to play before, which take more than our usual creativity. Thinking about each shot as a new creation is a very positive approach to shot making.

This is another good break point in your reading. Get out the CD and do Exercise 3, the first meditation exercise.

OTHER C-WORDS

Other words, also beginning with the letter C, may be more important to you and your game. *Competent, challenging, courageous, complete* and *childlike* are examples that could be made into affirmations. (My image of *childlike* by the way, is a youngster playing games with abandonment and joy). But not all focus words in golf begin with the letter C, so a friend adds the C-word *capable* to keep the idea of C-words going. For his golf he makes up affirmations such as, "I am capable of finding and main-taining my best tempo." An example I have used effec-tively during a game is, "I am capable of chipping this ball close."

Each meditation exercise stresses muscle relaxation because it is important in golf. I also emphasize the idea of control in each exercise. Your meditations, repeating the suggestion of being relaxed in a controlled way, will make this image part of your golf game. They will also spill over into your everyday activities and ease job-related stress. I do not have a meditation on concentra-tion because each exercise involves you becoming absorbed in the ideas and the images I have chosen. This – being absorbed – is the essence of concentration.

WANDERING THOUGHTS

When you meditate, your thoughts may wander. When that happens there's a natural tendency to try to force your brain back on track – and forcing yourself to think along certain paths is the exact opposite of what we want to achieve. So allow the wandering thoughts to go on. Don't fight them. Just allow the main thought to come back into your focus easily and naturally, helped by repeating the focus word. Simply allow yourself to be captured, to become absorbed in the images of the meditation.

If outside noises – like music or chatter – intrude, change the way you process the noise. Rather than let yourself become involved in the meaning of the words, focus on the sounds and use these to deepen the meditation. Allow the rhythm of the music or the talking to form the background to your imaging, and continue to meditate in a passive, accepting way. Practice this a few times, and then transfer the skill to the golf course. When you process noises or movements in this way, your level of concentration on your shot will become more acute. To prepare for a tournament, practice for it by asking your partners to talk or move during your shots in casual rounds and you soon become expert at refocusing in the face of distraction.

To be really useful, meditation requires practice, so you need to develop the daily practice habit. For some people, frequent shorter periods of daydreaming about golf, particularly when you direct the dreams, may be equally effective. For example, commit to two weeks of twice-daily daydreaming-like practice. You're making several four-foot putts and you focus on the feel of your head being still, until you hear the ball fall into the cup.

We all daydream, just as we dream during our night-time sleep. And our brains handle daydreams in more or less the same way as they do our nighttime dream cycles. It's as if the brain needs a rest from its usual analytical and logical mode of functioning so it refreshes itself by slipping into a daytime dream that lasts about twenty minutes. When it does, it changes its control system and allows body organs to go into their resting mode. That is why we often yawn and stretch after a daydream, although we haven't been to sleep. And daydreams are very much like meditative states. You could say that you're halfway into a meditation, so a portion of the time could be used to reinforce your positive images in golf. (There's more on daydreams in Appendix B, *Ultradian rhythms*.)

RIGHT-BRAIN/LEFT-BRAIN THEORY

In the meditative state (altered mode), we treat ideas in a somewhat different way from what we do when we're in our usual or dominant mode of functioning. In the altered state, we rely more on intuition and we tend to view the whole idea (right-brain), rather than analyse each part separately (left-brain).

You know those times, when the more you work at solving a problem the closer you seem to get to it, until you can't see the wood for the trees? So you walk away and forget it for a while. Then when you come back to it later, in a flash there's a solution to the whole thing. Your first thinking process is analytical and left-brain, but when you come back to it and see it as a complete picture your right brain handles it as a whole.

There has been a lot of research into the theory and application of the idea of different left- and right-brain activity. Whatever the reasons for it happening – and there is no hard and fast proof of why it works this way – all the evidence shows that it does happen. And one thing we do know is that the right brain is more active during a peak performance, which is why it's so important when we play golf.

In simple terms:

- The left side of the brain is analytical and logical. It processes information sequentially in units, and it uses words as its mode of expression.

- The right side is spatial and intuitive. It processes information simultaneously and holistically (a word that has come to mean the putting together all parts of an idea, or a problem, into one package). It uses images as its mode of expression.

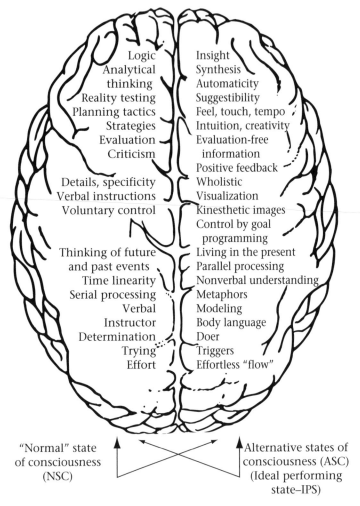

Logic
Analytical
thinking
Reality testing
Planning tactics
Strategies
Evaluation
Criticism

Insight
Synthesis
Automaticity
Suggestibility
Feel, touch, tempo
Intuition, creativity
Evaluation-free
information
Positive feedback

Details, specificity
Verbal instructions
Voluntary control

Wholistic
Visualization
Kinesthetic images
Control by goal
programming

Thinking of future
and past events
Time linearity
Serial processing
Verbal
Instructor
Determination
Trying
Effort

Living in the present
Parallel processing
Nonverbal understanding
Metaphors
Modeling
Body language
Doer
Triggers
Effortless "flow"

"Normal" state
of consciousness
(NSC)

Alternative states of
consciousness (ASC)
(Ideal performing
state–IPS)

Figure 1. The contrasting functions attributed to the right/left brain.

You can test this idea by describing in words a golf swing that you have just made. Then do the same using images of what you felt, saw and heard as you were making the swing. I think you will find that it's easier to do with images. And this contrast may be one reason why it is difficult to teach and to learn a physical skill such as the golf swing.

Although we do need to know facts and principles to understand the golf swing, the learner also has to translate a wordy description of a skill into their own images and sensations. It probably comes as no surprise to learn that the best human performances happen when the functions of both sides of the brain work together as one. The trouble is that we naturally tend to rely on the left side and use it more. We have to work at getting the most from the right side, which is why you see it mentioned fairly often throughout the program.

So think about making a golf shot, and consider what it means in terms of right- and left-brain function.

The left-brain activity begins when you consider the target, the weather and the hazards. You look at any slope, the sort of grass, the lie. Then you plan the shot, select the club, step up to the ball and take your stance in relation to the target. At this point, you shift to right-brain activity. You visualize the flight of the ball to the target, form a kinesthetic image by "feeling" the movements of the stroke, and then make the shot with this single narrow focus of attention.

I chose two model meditation exercises: Committed and Confidence. These particular C-words are linked to positive outcomes. Meditating on these focus words will counter those negative thoughts that can get in the way of the golf you are capable of playing.

You can narrow these down to just one word as my friend Philip does, because the word, Committed, embodies the other ideas for him. The affirmation then becomes "I am committed to allowing myself to become absorbed in this task, to strive to make my best shot, to be confident I can do it …" etc.

CHAPTER SUMMARY

It is important to understand the influence of self-criticism and negative self-talk, and what happens when we give ourselves negative expectations, such as, "I never make these three-foot putts." It is far more productive to think success rather than failure. As a general rule, when you imagine the shot facing you, you should imagine ideal shot making. For example, "I can make these three-foot putts in all circumstances." Or, "I am *confident.* I look forward to the *challenge* of this shot."

LIFE OUTSIDE GOLF

If certain situations make you nervous – maybe speaking in a meeting or even in smaller groups – take a few moments to recall a less stressful, similar situation and savour the feeling of confidence you had when you expressed yourself easily and comfortably.

Then use an affirmation that evokes these feelings, and say it quietly to yourself as you approach the situation that made you nervous.

This is another break point in your reading. Take a few minutes to listen and do the next meditation exercise. Exercise 4 on Confidence would be appropriate at this stage of the program.

C H A P T E R   S I X

ACTIVATION VERSUS RELAXATION

"It's not a question of getting rid of butterflies,
it's a question of getting them to fly in formation."
— *Jack Donohue, Canadian*
Olympic Basketball Team coach

LOSING ACTIVE RELAXATION

You will recognize this situation, because we have all been there. You stand on the tee with a good score going, but there are three other groups waiting ahead of you on the tee. You're ready to play, but forced to wait. You feel you may lose your rhythm. You become bored and wonder if you can prepare for the tee shot before cooling down too much. You are too relaxed, so you think about how to psyche yourself, reactivate yourself to continue to play well.

Exercise 5 gives you one way of doing this. You take three deep breaths using your diaphragm and chest wall muscles to open up the outer reaches of your lungs – those parts of the lungs that usually rest when you're breathing quietly. Then you use the imagery of blood, now loaded with oxygen from the deep breaths, flowing to your muscles and brain, to prepare yourself for your best effort for the shot you face and for the rest of the game. This can move you back into your actively relaxed state. It can energize you while maintaining the balance with relaxation.

But be careful – if you keep up deep breathing you can easily upset the electrolyte balance in your blood by getting rid of too much carbon dioxide. That can make you feel dizzy and faint.

Several studies show that the level of activation that produces the best performances is just below the point

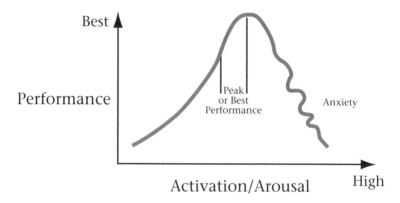

Figure 2: The stylised inverted U curve shows the relationship between activation/ arousal and performance. The line becomes irregular once it is past the peak, to indicate that it is difficult to move back once anxiety symptoms develop.

where anxiety develops. So we need some stress but not too much. The relationship between activation and athletic performance is usually illustrated as a sort of upside-down U curve, in Figure 2. It shows that increasing activation is good for performance – but only up to a certain level of activation. Take the activation past that point and it starts to become negative, developing into anxiety. When this happens performance suffers or breaks down entirely. And by far the best way to get back to the correct level of active relaxation – just below the critical level – is by using your inner mental skills (see Figure 2.)

The curve in Figure 2 is true for all sports and performances. For sprinters or weightlifters, who need a high level of activation to explode into action, the curve starts more to the right on the arousal scale. With golf the curve starts closer to the left side of the arousal scale, because golf requires less activation to perform well.

THE FIGHT-OR-FLIGHT RESPONSE

Activation is when we feel excited as we anticipate what's coming. The excitement is the result of our thoughts as they stimulate the release of hormones like adrenaline and cortisone. These chemicals our body releases raise the heartbeat, make our breathing deeper and more rapid, focus the mind very sharply and increase our strength and energy. Blood is diverted from the digestive system to the muscles and the brain, to prepare for a burst of physical and mental activity. The heart pumps more blood with each beat and blood pressure rises. This is the sympathetic stress response … fight-or-flight.

It's called fight-or-flight because they're the body's two natural options when we face danger. Come across a snarling dog and we feel all these symptoms, because our body is preparing us to either fight it or run from it. Whichever we go for, we need extra energy, strength and speed – a short burst so we can hit it harder than we would normally be able to, or run faster than usual.

Athletes in team sports like Ice Hockey know these symptoms and feelings very well. They enjoy the feelings and call it being pumped up, or say, "The adrenaline was really flowing."

So it is a useful physiological reaction … as long as it does not go too far. When the symptoms become excessive, we lose balance and things become chaotic. Our heart rate becomes too fast, breathing becomes irregular, and our muscles seem to lock up and won't work smoothly. Most of us recognize these symptoms from situations that have frightened us. Most of us have experienced it standing on the first tee, preparing to drive with several people watching. Your heart rate jumps, your mouth dries up and your hands feel moist, shaky and unsteady. You may even tremble a bit.

For anyone with a phobia, these symptoms can reach alarming levels and can deeply affect their ability to perform. A phobia is an exaggerated fear reaction to a situation or object that most people accept as ordinary. There are phobias in golf – maybe the most common example is the putting yips, which can be so severe that the putter blade feels frozen to the green, and the stroke becomes a jab.

The good news is that the putting yips is generally a learned reaction. So the sufferer can relearn the response and eliminate the problem with a combination of relaxation and imagery.

MODIFYING YOUR REACTION TO FIGHT-OR-FLIGHT

We used to think the fight-or-flight response was automatic and out of our control – a basic survival instinct. But you can use the meditative state and learn to control the symptoms, to strike just the right level of activation for the task you face.

You do this using the skills learned so far, to slow your heart rate, alter your breathing pattern, and lower the level of tension in your muscles. If you were a computer, you would be reprogramming the software in your brain. By controlling the symptoms of anxiety you control the level of the fight-or-flight reflex.

CONTROLLING YOUR BODY'S RESPONSES

Exercise 5, on activation, provides you with images to increase blood flow to your hands and fingers, and to test your progress you'll need a digital thermometer.

Hold the sensor tip of the thermometer in the web between your thumb and index finger and take a reading. If the reading you get is below the lowest temperature on its scale, make a note of where the indicator was, so you can see the difference.

Do Exercise 5 and then take another reading. During this exercise, I provide suggestions and images to increase blood flow to your fingers. Your finger temperature will go up by a degree or more because of the increased blood flow to your fingers.

I suggest you stop reading at this point, get the CD and do Exercise 5 while these ideas are fresh in your mind.

Using the technique for golf

This exercise will help you play better golf in more extreme weather conditions. So, on a cool, rainy day when the outside temperature drops, the body's reflex is to reduce blood flow to the skin, to preserve body heat.

You are learning to modify this "cold reflex" using your alternate mode of control, with suggestions and images that cause the walls of blood vessels supplying the skin to relax. This will increase blood flow to the skin (where the body's temperature sensors are) and modify the heat-preserving reflex. It's like raising the thermostat in your house to increase the heat output from the central heating.

You can also produce the opposite effect, for playing in very warm weather. For some people, perspiration can be a real problem when they're trying to grip and swing with confidence. So learn to control this reflex by creating images that make your sweat glands slow down production. Decrease the blood flow to the sweat glands by creating suggestions to increase the tone of the muscles of the walls of the arteries to the glands. Your body will ensure that there is just enough sweat to evaporate and cool the body.

Using your self-hypnosis skills like this can give you control over many unpleasant situations. Create and practice them in your imagination before you have to use them in real life. In this way, you are ready for the situation when it does develop.

CHAPTER SUMMARY

It is important that you can activate yourself and become aware of the feelings associated with the correct level of activation. Use imagery and suggestions to establish the right balance of activation and relaxation, for a good performance. Use your altered state during meditation, to tune into your body's response to different situations you've experienced in real life. You can then learn when a muscle is properly prepared for action, either as the active muscle or as the opposing one that makes the action smooth as it allows itself to lengthen.

LIFE OUTSIDE GOLF

Use the simple energizing breathing imagery to prepare for situations like attending a meeting when you are tired, and where you need to psyche yourself up for an important event.

Another common problem is excess saliva while the dentist is working on your teeth. While you are waiting to go in, use your mental skills to develop the altered state and create the image of your mouth as dry, almost dehydrated. Reduced saliva means less swallowing and so less discomfort while the dentist works on your teeth.

CHAPTER SEVEN

SETTING GOALS TO IMPROVE YOUR GOLF

"Today's goals are tomorrow's realities."

– *Terry Orlick*

SETTING AND REASSESSING YOUR GOALS

The fact that you are interested in this program suggests you have a goal, even if it's just a general desire to satisfy your curiosity about *Golf: Lower Your Score With Mental Training* and find out, "What could inner mental training do for me?"

In every field of human activity, research into goal setting has reinforced what every outstanding athlete knows instinctively, that setting goals improves performance.

Specifically:

- Working toward a goal improves self-confidence and motivation, and at the same time reduces anxiety.

- Performance goals – playing to personal standards you set for yourself – are more effective than outcome goals (like winning a tournament or match). So consistent shot making that gives you second place, is better than a fluke that wins it for you.

- People who create images of themselves as having achieved their goals are more likely to reach them.

Athletes need the motivation of wanting to win. But focusing on winning a competition is far less effective than concentrating on performing at their best. On the golf course, you can only play as well as you can. You can't win by controlling an opponent's play, but you can lose if you start trying to beat them instead of using mental skills to play each shot well, and play your own game.

So goal-setting begins by knowing your present situation. Develop a picture, or write a description of where you are now. Then develop a picture of the level of play you would like to achieve. That's your goal, and it doesn't have to be hugely difficult. For some people, it would be sufficient to play well enough with friends without looking like a complete novice every time. For most golfers though, it will be about improved shot-making, better scores or a lower handicap.

A diary really helps

Keeping a diary of your games and your practice sessions is an excellent way to develop and assess performance goals. It will pinpoint the parts of your game that need improvement. It also tells you whether goals are being achieved and whether they need updating.

There's a model diary in Appendix A, along with more details. The model uses an ordinary scorecard to make notes of your different shots in the game. So these notes not only give you a statistical record of your games, they also act as a reminder about your mental game. The model highlights the different parts of the game, helping you to assess your game and update your goals.

But because we know that positive thinking is beneficial while negative thoughts can be damaging, the first statistic you work out relates to all the good shots in the game.

PERFORMANCE GOALS

Not everyone likes setting goals. You may think it looks like too much of a hassle, a trendy management fad. Besides, they can be negative too, surely? How does one handle failing to achieve a goal?

Dr Terry Orlick says that self-acceptance is the most overlooked aspect in the process of setting goals. In his extensive experience with athletes, he has never met one who intentionally messed up a performance. So your first goal should be to like yourself, to see yourself as a good person who can and will learn from every experience, whether it's a good one or one that is not up to your standards.

Remember – it's important to make the very important distinction between a performance goal and an outcome goal. The problem with outcome goals is that you can control your own performance, but you can't control the performance of others, the weather or a rub of the green. You can play your best ever round and lose to someone else who does exactly the same.

You can roughly divide performance goals into short-, medium- and long-term. And there are a few things to bear in mind as you set and work with your performance goals.

MAKE THEM REALISTIC

Even some tour players would have difficulty with this one; it's a wish rather than a goal:

Make 20 out of 20 10-foot putts. Start again if you miss one putt, and don't leave the practice green until you have reached that goal.

Fatigue or a sore back – or darkness when night falls – may cause mistakes. There is no point in trying to work through them by practicing those mistakes until you are exhausted. It is wiser to take time off from physical practice and use the meditative state to review images of your best putting games and compare them to your present practice. That will expose errors that have crept into your swing – the first step in correcting them.

So instead of an unrealistic wish, set a realistic goal. Make it specific and short-term.

I will make…

- *… 10 of 10 putts from 12 to 18 inches*
- *… 9 of 10 from 2 feet*
- *… 7 of 10 from 3 feet*
- *… 6 of 10 putts from 5 feet*

(Even the pros don't make 100% of 5-footers!).

The diary section (Appendix A) explains more about breaking your game down into its various parts ... putting, chipping and so on. If you set separate short-term goals for chipping and putting, they could both be part of a medium-term goal – to lower your short-game scores.

Achieving successive goals like these improve your chances of making it to a longer-term goal, such as a lower handicap within a certain time limit.

MAKE THEM ACHIEVABLE

Make you performance goals specific and measurable. Keep them simple and make them challenging but achievable. They must be an improvement on our present performance, high enough to be challenging and realistic enough to be achievable. In Chapter Three, I talked about our inner coach, the part of us that knows our strengths and weaknesses very well. So for most of us goals like ... *I will get down to scratch by the end of the year,* are not only pointless, they are demotivating. We know we won't do it, so we give up before we even start.

Begin with a few relatively easy short-term goals. It boosts your morale as you work toward a long-term goal, and it keeps goal setting in perspective and keeps you focused on progress. Stick to the idea that a goal must motivate, not rule your life.

MAKE THEM PROGRESSIVE

Start with an achievable standard and then improve on it so, for example, start with a goal of ten shots landing anywhere on the green, when playing from sixty yards out. Then reduce the target area for the next ten shots by a few yards … and then reduce it again. If you keep a record, you can easily record progress as percentages. And using ten or so balls at a time gives you the chance to rest between sets. That is better than just pitching balls from the same spot until you have a perfect score, and it makes it easier to keep making progress on the same goal, on different days.

REVIEW YOUR PROGRESS

Your inner coach can guide you and help to set, review and reassess your goals.

Write down long-term and intermediate goals. Express them in the present tense, in positive terms, and in words that create an image of you achieving the goal. Be as wordy as you like to start with, then rewrite your goals in progressively shorter forms, until they're just a word or two long. These then become your power words, your affirmation phrases.

Motivate yourself by setting realistic target dates. Review your progress and your goals regularly. It gives you a reference point to work to, and it also lets you check that your goals are reality rather than fantasy, and whether you need to revise them.

No matter how a performance turns out, if you do not meet a well-thought-out and realistic goal, you will feel sadness and disappointment. But do not wallow in failure. You do not have failures, you only have experiences from which come continuous self-improvement. Disappointment is an experience to learn from, so don't beat yourself up for not doing as well as you hoped, and then set about learning from the experience.

Think about what you have done well, and use those experiences as triggers, images and positive memories. Then identify where you didn't do as well as you had expected, and use those images to improve in those areas.

IMAGING GOAL ACHIEVEMENT

More and more tour golfers have a mind coach as well as a swing coach. One of the things they focus on is visualization – seeing themselves achieving their goals.

Olympic athletes practice the same thing. Sylvie Bernier, in the last few weeks before she won her gold medal in diving at the 1984 Olympics, spent most of her training time practicing imagery away from the diving pool. She visualized perfect dives in each category. These were her performance goals.

There's a video – *Visualization, What You See Is What You Get* – that shows her standing quietly on the board … eyes closed, focused on her internal images, then moving smoothly into her dives. In it she describes how she practiced the images of her outcome goal in each of her sense systems. She saw herself walking along the pool to the podium, heard the applause of the crowd, and felt the medal being placed around her neck.

Greg Louganis, another gold-medal-winning diver, added a further step in this method. He took the time after each and every really good dive – in practice or in competition – to savour and relish the feelings of making a perfect dive. The result is that whenever he thinks about his dives, the dominant emotions are the good feelings of his best dives.

There is no one exercise imagining having achieved a goal. Rather, I have included the suggestion in each of the meditation exercises (Exercises 3 and 4), you are asked to create an image of yourself having achieved the goal of playing with confidence, or with the easy-flowing commitment of good shot-making.

Be creative in your imaging. Use the video screen in your inner mental room to create and practice the moving image of yourself achieving your goals as in the above examples. Be an observer at first. Watch the video of your success to get in as much detail as possible. Then rerun the video, but this time be the actor as well. This is easy to do in the image mode and it lets you create these very important visceral images, feeling the joys of success, when you have done well. Remember to add sound to the video to hear the compliments when you make those good shots!

I cannot stress too much that the best foundation for improving your shot making is positive feedback from the good parts of your golf game. Do what Greg Louganis does and visualize and feel the movements of your good shots, both in practice and on the course. Relish the satisfaction and the thrill of a well-played shot. Make these feeling memories the most important emotions attached to the images of your shots.

CHAPTER SUMMARY

Setting performance goals for yourself is an excellent way to improve your golf game. Set performance goals and not outcome goals. Make them realistic, achievable and progressive. Start by making short-term goals in putting and chipping, where results come quickly. Increase the difficulty of the goals as outlined in the example above. Motivate yourself by assigning specific dates to achieve your goals and review your progress. See a missed goal as a learning opportunity, never as a failure.

LIFE OUTSIDE GOLF

You can use goals to help you achieve a sense of balance in your life. Consider what is important in your life when planning goals. Do I really want this goal? What will achieving this goal do to my lifestyle? What will the process of achieving it do to my family, my work, my income, my spiritual health, my self-esteem, my physical health, and my important relationships?

CHAPTER EIGHT

PROBLEM SOLVING WITH CREATIVE IMAGERY

"I can change! You can change!
Everybody can certainly change!"

– Rocky IV

"From the ancient 'to be or not to be,' to the present
'to become or not to become!' "

– Lars Eric Uneståhl

CHANGING A REACTION HABIT

If you say, "I always go in the lake on this hole," and replace your regular ball with an old one you don't mind losing … you will go in the lake. You have seriously reinforced the negative image and increased the chances that the ball will end up in the water. You are encouraging a pattern, a habit of negative reaction.

Then, if your reaction to poor shots is frustration and anger at yourself, you run the risk of generating high levels of the messenger molecules that go with the fight-or-flight response. That stresses you straightaway, and the angry feelings usually last for several holes while the body takes its time dealing with the chemicals. And of course there's a store of them, ready to make it even worse when you next face a small pond or stream.

Fortunately, there is a way to change this kind of habitual response to frustration or anger. You can use your inner mental skills to remember what happened and learn from it … to change habitual thoughts or reactions that interfere with your performance.

After a badly played hole or a three- or four-putt green, golfers often say, "I lost my concentration." My first seminar group worked out a method for surviving such a setback. They said, acknowledge the error because this allows you to view the mistake more objectively. Then review the event in your mind, from both the mental and physical standpoints. And replay the shot in your mind as it should have been played.

FORGIVE, REMEMBER AND LEARN

Here is a simulation to learn this idea. You can of course use your mental room to help visualize the scene. The scene is this. You have just thinned a chip shot over the green, a shot you usually take for granted. You now face another chip shot, and perhaps your ball is in a worse lie than the first.

Your normal reaction would be to feel rattled, and if you allowed yourself to be angry with yourself for poor shots, you'd be disgusted with yourself and your performance.

This exercise combines the original ideas that came from my first group of students, with the added new step of forgiveness.

- Acknowledge the error or errors. This makes the error less personal, like putting it out on the table to be examined.

- Forgive yourself for making the error. This is a simple thought that allows you to look at the error more objectively. (You'd quickly forgive your golf partner for making the same mistake, wouldn't you? After all, you'd know it was the last thing they wanted to do, and you would try to stop them feeling bad.)

- As you walk to your next shot, reflect on the error, looking at both mental and physical aspects. In the image mode, walk through the incident as you would have liked to play the shot. In the meditative state, this is a very quick, unobtrusive process because imagery is used.

- Accept the challenge of the shot, rehearse how you would like to play the shot, and then play it with confidence.

- Remember the experience and benefit from it.

Learn to laugh at yourself

The ability to truly laugh at yourself is one of the best ways to dissipate anger associated with your reaction to error.

Medical students learn their interviewing skills through a video playback of their history talking with an "actor patient". When they see the video afterwards they often laugh at their mistakes and behaviour. This is a great idea because laughing at yourself can spur you on to change. When you are the actor on the TV screen of your imagination, you often see the humour in the situation. This helps to change your perception of your performances.

So if you can learn to laugh rather than get angry, you are more likely to use the experience as a learning opportunity.

BREAK THE REACTION HABIT

This is a pattern that builds on the idea *Forgive, remember and learn*. You can use it to stop the negative reactions developing into habits and patterns.

- Acknowledge that the performance was not what you had expected.

- Accept that you do not always make perfect shots.

- Reflect – were you not quite ready to make the shot … were you distracted by a doubt, like "Have I got the wrong club for this shot"? When you use imagery, this process is very quick. And no one knows what you are doing when you quietly look at the ground for a moment, then walk purposefully to the next shot. By this time the negative feelings have dissipated and you're ready for the challenge of the next shot.

- As you prepare for the next shot, work in the feeling of readiness that accompanies your affirmation. For example, "I am fully committed to this club and this shot."

- Finally, replay the shot in your mind as you would want to have played it, confidently creating a good shot. This positive image will interfere with the memory process. The new image will block out the negative one and neither will get into your long-term memory. The method works so well that I suggest you write down your score at the time. If you don't, you could well have difficulty remembering it a few holes later.

This reflective process reduces the number of messenger molecules your body produces as a reaction to an error. Over time, the level of the stored messenger molecules falls as well. And the habitual self-anger diminishes because it now takes a much stronger stimulus to generate a forceful reaction to minor errors.

Incidentally, you may have noticed that I am talking about errors, not failures. They are not the same. Errors and good shots are both experiences to be learned from. We often forget that we learn from the good things as much as – or more than – we do from our errors. So always pay attention to how well you handle challenges, as a positive strand in your strategy for preventing problems from arising or developing.

TAKING RECURRING PROBLEMS OUT OF YOUR GAME

Most golfers seem to have at least one problematic hole or shot ... often a particular tee shot. The problem is that we expect to play a poor shot on that tee, and that expectation is the key. Taking your stance, you feel a little anxious and tense and more aware of hazards than usual. The image you have in focus is the shot going astray, so more often than not, your shot does that, just as you'd expect.

You can use your imaging capability to manage this and other similar problems. Exercise 6 teaches you to use your imaging capability to manage problems. In this example, it's when you have a recurring problem tee-shot, a short hole over a water hazard.[3] I hope that this common problem can serve as a model to manage other mental problems in your game. Follow the exercise on Track 7, but change the directions a little to fit this description. Here is the new procedure:

Exercise 6 is a Neuro-Linguistic Programming (NLP) Technique called the SWISH Pattern.

Here are the steps involved. On the CD, we will do these using a simulation, but an outline like this will prepare you for the process:

1. Identify the problem state. Go into a light trance by taking a breath and making fists, then let your breath go, as you relax into your meditative state, to

---

3. Exercise 6 is a neuro-linguistic programming (NLP) "Swish" technique. This description is an elaboration and follows a Gary Faris example of a skier. He points out that athletes always look to a future performance. Scene B is a future performance. When you listen to Exercise 6, you must make Scene B a future event.

better use your imaging capability. Focus on the undesired behaviour and your response to it.

2. Be specific. What do you see yourself doing through your own eyes, what do you hear through your own ears, and, most important, what sensations do you have – what do you feel? Make this picture sharp, bright and colourful. Call this image Picture A and tuck it away in your memory while you do the next step.

3. Identify the desired state you need to play the shot you know you can make. Make a picture of what you would see, what you would hear, and again the most important item, what feelings, what sensations you would experience in the desired state. Call this Picture B.

4. What resources do you have to access the physical capability you know you have to play the shot as it needs to be played? The relaxation level, the intensity of the focus you will need to move from the

problem state to the desired state. Tap your inner coach for help to access these resources. Make a picture of yourself having these resources and behaviours. But place it outside yourself, that is, you will be watching yourself perform with the new resources. Make this picture dim and small. Place it in the corner of the screen in your mind.

5. Before proceeding to the actual Swish, go further inside yourself and check to see if any part of you does not agree with this picture. Would this be an arrogant you, unacceptable to your view of yourself? Or would a part of you miss the feeling of being a victim, and the complaining that goes with it? If so, then you have the opportunity to change the picture to allow for that concern.

6. Now proceed with the Swish that consists of replacing Picture A with Picture B – Picture B will fill the screen as Picture A fades into the distance.

We will do this exercise with the CD, but first some words of caution:

- Be sure the technique is working for you. Do a few practice run-throughs and be sure that you have good images of Scenes A and B and that Picture B does replace Picture A.

- Repetition is important; so you must do five repetitions each time. If you want to do more at the same sitting, pause between sets of five repetitions. You should not do more than four sets at one time. Do the remainder at another time of the day.

- Always go from A to B, stop and clear your mind by opening your eyes and glancing to one side or just make the screen blank. Remember that you do not wish to have the undesired state as the last picture in your mind, as would happen if you went A-B-A-B-A.

- Remember that in the image mode, your brain works very fast, so the faster the change of scenes, the better. So, if you wish to reinforce the new you just before making your shot, you can do a quick Swish. Then, when you have that Picture B in your mind, you can do what Philip Perry does; imagine it has a magnet that draws you into itself as you move up to make the shot, so that you become the person in the picture.

You should do sets of five in each session and do several sessions each day. You will see that it becomes increasingly difficult to recall Scene A, or it becomes less sharp. There will come a point when the experience of not having the problem in real life takes over. You can then stop doing the exercise.

However, problems like this do tend to reappear, and the reason for paying attention to the body sensations at the start of Scene A is that these sensations can be the first clue that the problem is trying to make a come-back. You can then take a moment of your pre-shot routine to run the exercise again a few times, since it takes just a few moments and nobody around you will notice.

Listen to and do Exercise 6 while these ideas are fresh in your mind.

COMBINE THE CHANGED MENTAL SET WITH PHYSICAL PRACTICE

Now that you have raised your feelings of confident expectation, you can take them to your next practice putting session and follow this pattern to reinforce the change. Here is how I go through a putting practice, combining the physical with the mental practice:

- Set goals for each practice session and each distance as outlined in Chapter Seven. Review and set higher goals as you improve.

- Set three balls about a foot away from the hole and push the balls to the hole to get the feel of the putter head going to the hole (this is an important move in putting).

- Then stroke the balls from the same distance until you are satisfied with the results. Be sure to keep the putter head going to the hole as before. Set the balls far enough apart so that you have to set up each time as if in a game, rather than bring the balls to where you are standing.

- Repeat the sequence of three balls from two, three, four and five feet. Line up the longer putts and force yourself to go through your full putting routine, even if it's just in your mind.

- Putting to different targets at different distances sharpens your feel for distance. Pick targets on the green, look at the target for at least two seconds, then follow the line of the putt back to your putter. Then, trusting in your ability to feel the distance, make the stroke. Focus on making the putter head go along your chosen line, rather than on hitting the ball.

- Stop occasionally and review your mental strategy for putting. Hopefully, you have reviewed these strategies when in your mental room and then used them in your practice putting sessions.

ANOTHER IMAGE FOR PUTTING

When I putt, I use an image I borrowed from martial-arts practitioners, to help focus less on the ball and more on the distance and line. They break boards with their bare hands but they don't focus on the board. Their image is of their hand arriving well below the board. So rather than look at the ball as I stroke the putt, I imagine the line of the putt underneath the ball, or in front of or behind the ball. Then I make the putter head go through the ball along that line to the hole.

You may have to soften your eyes – defocus as you imagine the putter travelling along the line. One interesting result of this action is that it helps you to relax, because you are relaxing the muscle that focuses the lens of your eye. You can use this action as the trigger to develop the active relaxation needed to putt well.

The ball now becomes much less important, and the images more important. As you concentrate on images of the process, you are less interested in hitting the ball and more involved in what you want to achieve, stroking the ball to your target. Of course, this helps to keep your body quiet through the stroke – the undisputed mark of a good putter.

IMPROVING MY OWN PUTTING

Dr Joan Vickers of the University of Calgary's Department of Kinesiology's Neuro-Motor Psychology Laboratory studies athletes involved in static-type sports activities like putting, basketball free throw, rifle shooting and pool. These are activities that allow easy access for instruments to measure some functions, in this case eye movements and brain activity. In *Golf Magazine* (October

1991), she published a short description of what good putters do, compared to poor putters.

After lining up the putt and checking it once, the good putters focused on the hole for at least two seconds. They then traced the path of the ball back to the ball itself and stroked the ball with very little hesitation. I was already doing that, except for the time looking at the target and the time spent tracing the path back to the ball. Once I adopted those techniques, my putting became even more successful, particularly for distance and direction on longer putts.

A few weeks later, I tried a little experiment with my grandson and three of his friends, all about thirteen years old with little or no golf experience. We were on the practice green and at first they seemed to have no idea where their putts were going. So I asked them to look at the target for two full seconds – which is a surprisingly long time when you first try it – before hitting the ball. They were thrilled with the results and although it's not a scientific experiment, it convinced me to carry on doing it in my own putting. I've also adopted it for chipping and improved my distance judgment.

Dr Vickers is still doing her research and had an article in the January 2004 issue of *Golf Digest* entitled "The Quiet Eye". In it she advocates also looking at one spot on the ball for two seconds before stroking the ball. Now, I have some difficulty with this particular advice, even though most golfers glance quickly and repeatedly at the target as part of their routines. I think that concentrating on a spot on the ball has the potential to disturb concentration on the target. To me, concentration is a flowing activity that can suffer if you try to change your focus and use an essentially left-brain action to pick a spot on the ball. I believe it's better to trust your stroke and stay absorbed in the images of what you wish to achieve.

One final point about stamina

When you're practicing, beware of fatigue. Never be afraid to rest, or even to quit if you start to make errors because you are getting bored with repetition, or your back aches from the putting posture. As part of your rest from practice, review the physical and mental routines of your putting. Remember that you want to recall the image of success when putting under stress, like sinking that last putt to make your best score ever.

After all, this is why you play the game – to enjoy yourself, to feel good about your performance, to feel good about yourself. When you expect to feel good about your game, lower scores will follow.

CHAPTER SUMMARY

Most golfers have one or two recurring problem situations in their game, a shot over water, or out of sand, or
a particular tee shot. Each time they are faced with the
shot, their anxiety level rises; negative expectations
rattle around in their minds, and a disastrous effort
often follows. Remember the value of affirmations.
Practice the techniques to reprogram the software in
your brain, to change negative expectations to images of
successful, well-played shots. If affirmations are not
effective, or the problem worsens, design a solution
around the ideas in Exercise 6. Use your meditative
state to pay particular attention to the body sensations
that accompany the beginning of the problem state.
Then write a detailed description of your present state
(the problem). Then do the same with the desired state.
Writing these detailed descriptions will enable you to
create "sharp, bright and detailed scenes" on your own
to substitute those in my script in Exercise 6.

LIFE OUTSIDE GOLF

Golf is one of the better sport metaphors for life. Many recurring situations in ordinary life are also anxiety producing. Like similar golf situations, each time they recur they are accompanied by a rising feeling of anxiety. Write a script on a minor recurring problem and then follow the method outlined in Exercise 6.

CHAPTER NINE

REACHING FOR A BEST PERFORMANCE

"Peak performers from various fields maintain their childlike qualities!"

– Lars Eric Uneståhl

PLAYING IN THE ZONE

Peak performances can occur in any human activity. They happen in creative activities, problem solving, in business presentations, volleyball or a piano concert. It is a phenomenon that has been studied in athletes, in all sports. They often call it being *in the zone,* and tour player Dave Barr said it was like playing in a glass tunnel, because he was aware of the crowds but unaffected by them. During peak experiences, one functions far above one's average level.

Surveys of athletes who have experienced a peak performance show several common characteristics, which involve the mind's control over the performance. The mental skills attained by these athletes are important for your golf game and are well worth emulating.

- *Self-image.* Play golf with relaxed self-confidence. Self-confidence is your responsibility. Beware of thinking, "I am confident because I am making good shots," because this implies that the only time you play with confidence is when things are going well.

- *Motivation.* Commit yourself to your standard of play and to your goals. Create images in all your sense systems to enhance the process: see yourself having achieved your goal; enjoy the physical feelings of success; hear the plaudits of your playing partners.

- *Attitude.* Everything that happens to you teaches you something about yourself. Errors are experiences to learn from, just like the experience of making a good shot.

- *Mood* (your mindset). Be optimistic and expect to play well. Practicing optimism can transform a habit of always expecting a bad shot.

THE IDEAL PERFORMANCE EXPERIENCE

Most of us have had a peak experience, perhaps playing a few holes of golf, or perhaps in another sport or activity altogether. As you did it you felt happily absorbed with what you were doing and did every task automatically, with little or no conscious effort. Afterwards, you knew that something was different, that it had been well above your typical good performance.

Ideal (or best) performance has been studied in many areas of human endeavour, perhaps most extensively in athletic performance. Athletes recognise that during these experiences, their mindset is different from their ordinary waking state. They describe it as "playing in the zone" or "playing in a cocoon". Dr Unestähl has interviewed athletes in many sports shortly after their best performances and has noticed how similar their descriptions were to descriptions of the self-hypnotic state. He uses the terms *ideal performance state* and *ideal performance feelings* to distinguish this part of the memory of a peak performance.

This more detailed account of a peak performance in golf illustrates these ideal performance feelings. Doug Brown was an assistant professional at my club and he described this peak performance to me a few hours after it happened. He was still wrapped up in the feelings of it that afternoon, after a local pro tour event at Redwood Meadows Golf Club, near Calgary.

> "I felt relaxed and confident when I woke up and had enough time for a comfortable drive to the course," he said. "My rhythm and tempo were nice and smooth on the practice range and green. After the first few holes, I became more aware of the good rhythm in my swing, and that my tempo remained

the same in every swing. I felt very confident in my ability to make good contact, and just let my ability work for me.

"Although I was four under par at the turn, and had missed makable putts on the previous two holes, I was not distracted by the score, and just thought about each shot as it came. I was aware that I was pumped up, that the adrenaline was flowing. Even when I went to six under on the twelfth hole, my anxiety level never changed. I was very relaxed and calm.

"On the 160-yard fifteenth, still feeling pumped up and very confident that I was striking the ball well, I decided to go with an eight iron. I don't usually hit an eight iron 160 yards, but I hit this one over the green on the fly into the hazard, and made a double bogey. This had no effect on my feeling of confidence, as I knew I had made a good shot. I remained calm and relaxed with no thought of failure. My pace, my sense of detachment, my rhythm and tempo remained the same throughout the whole day, for a very satisfying round of four under par."

He is describing a wonderful experience ... a round I am sure he dreams about repeating. However, reality dictates that no two shots are alike and no two games will ever be the same either. Peak performances are probably associated with the coming together of a number of bodily rhythms, so that one's body is at its absolute peak physically. This is why they appear irregularly and without warning, as Doug's did. Peak experiences may disappear too without warning as another pro golfer said when he described his experience with peak performance.

Dr Unestâhl found that his athletes who used inner mental training were more likely to have peak perform-ances, and were better able to sustain them when they did happen. These athletes accepted the peak experience without the negative thoughts that golfers often express – that they were playing out of their comfort zone, that playing well was sure to end with the next shot.

FEELING MEMORIES

There are many pleasant images in the memory of a peak performance. There is the sound of a putt dropping into the hole, the beautiful flight of the ball to the target, the tempo and the fluid motion of a swing repeated over and over. More important to the experience are the associated good feelings, the feeling memories so well described by Doug Brown.

I was introduced to the idea of recalling a peak performance at a hypnosis conference. The speaker asked each person in the audience to develop the altered state and then to access our memory bank to find a peak experience. I was pleasantly surprised to recall a flying experience that I hadn't thought of for years.

It happened during an end of course flight test, part of my RCAF elementary flying course in the summer of 1943. The little Tiger Moth seemed a part of me, an extension of myself. I performed each task the instructor gave me the best I had ever done. I hit the slipstream at the end of every turn and loop. The barrel rolls described a perfect circle around the point on the horizon. The landing was so smooth; I thought the wheels started to turn on the grass before touchdown.

You can probably tell from reading this description that I still have the feelings of the experience. I have had a few peak experiences in golf, and in each instance the feelings were identical to those of my flying experience.

In the simulation of Exercise 7, you learn to separate out the feeling memories of a peak experience. You can then focus on these feeling images, and project them into a game you play out in your mind – for example, a preview of an important game to be played the next day.

Bob McArthur, a young professional who was a member of my first series of seminars, used this technique and won most of the tournaments for assistant professionals that year. By itself, this technique will not guarantee a repeat peak performance, but it will improve your performance because you will expect to play confidently.

A sustained peak performance has other components too. You must be in good physical condition and have a good basic swing. You must also have well-trained inner mental skills.

Focusing on the very positive feelings associated with a previous ideal performance allows you to expect some errors, but because of your confident feelings you see such errors as bad luck or a rub-of-the-green. The errors will then have little or no effect on your confidence. This bold-spiritedness is the main aim of this program, what we want in golf and in life.

CREATE THE MEMORY OF A FUTURE PEAK PERFORMANCE

You will probably have had a peak experience in some activity at some point in your life. In Exercise 7, I ask you to recall such an experience when I lead you through a simulated experience. There may not be a memory of a whole peak experience game in your memory bank, but you are likely to have played a few holes in the best performance mode. Focus on the associated ideal performance feelings. Run the scene on the TV monitor in your mental room, again being both observer and actor to heighten your memory of the feelings.

Then comes the crucial part of the exercise. Create a memory of the future. I ask you to play each shot of an upcoming game on the monitor of your imagination, accompanied by the heightened feeling images of that peak performance. Continue to be both actor and observer to intensify the experience, to make it more real. Run the scene again with the aim of finding an anchor for the feelings. This will give you a fallback mechanism to help you recall your intense peak-performance feelings, in case they diminish in real-life situations.

Having done the recorded exercise, practice it on your own without my words. Take as much time as you need. Remember that in the altered mind state, you can speed up between shots and play the shots in slow motion to accentuate the feeling memories. If the memory doesn't come the first time you do the exercise, don't worry. It may take several sessions, and the recollection may surprise you at another quiet time outside of doing the exercise. When this happens in the altered state, you will be amazed at how sharp your memory is for these outstanding experiences.

Here is another point in your reading when you can take a break to listen and do Exercise 7, Peak Experience. Take as much time as you like to do this exercise, by simply carrying on with the experience after the CD ends.

THE IDEAL PERFORMANCE STATE

As explained earlier, the ideal performance state is very similar to the altered-mind state of meditation or hypnosis. These are some of the comparable features.

- You feel totally focused on your shots without trying. It may be like being in a glass tunnel – you are aware of your surroundings but the wall around you allows you to concentrate more easily.

- You have a sense that you are watching yourself perform, with no sense of fatigue or discomfort.

- You perceive things differently. For example, your swing may feel very slow, and you may feel as if you have used no real force in striking the ball, despite the distance and accuracy of the shot. Or you may perceive that the putt follows the exact path to the hole, that it just cannot miss. These changes in perception help you to expect and to make good shots.

- You experience great joy at the ease with which you are playing. The shots just flow naturally, as if the club were an extension of your body.

- You may have difficulty remembering the details of your best shots, but will have little trouble recalling details of the shot that went wrong. This is important because you must focus on the feelings associated with your best shots, not the details of the shot.

In this mind state, the right brain is allowed to dominate the process. Because most of us naturally relate to the dominant left-brain system of control, this alternative way of working takes time and energy to learn. We are not used to allowing effortless control. This is the key, the mindset for good performance.

Golf: Lower Your Score With Mental Training provides a structured, systematic method to learn the effortless control of good performance. A peak performance may only happen to you occasionally, but, when you experience one, you now have the skills to keep it going.

CHAPTER SUMMARY

Peak experiences occur in all walks of life. Golfers and other athletes say they "play in the zone". When asked specific questions about the experience, they relate feelings and perceptions very similar to those observations of people who have experienced the self-hypnotic state. Do practice your imagery capabilities using your altered state to relive the images of a previous peak experience, to help reinforce the trust in your capabilities.

To apply what you have learnt, play an important upcoming match or game in your mind. Play each shot with those wonderful feeling memories of the prior peak experience.

LIFE OUTSIDE GOLF

Transfer the images of an experience in one part of your life to another. For example, if a peak experience happened during a presentation at a meeting, then use the images in a memory of this event and play a future golf game with these feelings attached. Or use the images from a peak performance golf game for a speech you have to make at a wedding. Or vice versa!

A P P E N D I X   A

RECORDING YOUR MENTAL STRATEGIES

*"Each time you play a round of golf, you should use it
[your diary] to indicate the relative strengths and
weaknesses of your game."*

– Dr Bob Rotella

MAKING NOTES OF YOUR PROGRESS

All golfers make mental notes, a mental diary, of their
practice sessions and their games. Many know how many
greens they hit and most know how many putts they
took in the round. However, the process of writing a
diary or a logbook makes analysis easier, more thorough
and more objective. It also enhances the positive feelings
because you focus on improving smaller segments of

your game. If you do not play golf every day, a diary provides continuity. If you include practice sessions in the diary, the swing thoughts and routines you develop on the practice fairway transfer more easily to the course.

Start a logbook on inner mental training on the same day you start the exercises. A logbook can be a simple two-by-four-inch ring-bound booklet that you can carry in your pocket, so it's easily available, particularly when you use it at practice.

A line or two on your first experience with self-hypnosis can be about the experience itself. Were the images sharp? Did the garden scene fit a prior experience that you have had? (When I describe it on the compact disc, I have a combination of two public gardens in my mind.) Were you able to hear sounds in the scene clearly? (Interestingly, only about 10% of the population list hearing as their favourite sense system. The majority are visualizers.)

When practicing imagery, it is important to exercise all the senses, no matter which one is your favourite. This is because you heighten the imagery experience as you use more details in the image. In the PMR exercise, for example, if you find difficulty in feeling the muscles on the top of the forearm when you pull one hand back, the tendons rather than the muscles might feel tight. Note this.

Or use your free hand to feel the difference in firmness in these muscles as they work to bend the hand backward at the wrist, and make a note of this.

If you find a sequence that suits you better than mine, make a more detailed note of it and make the exercise your own, as I have done in rotating my torso during PMR.

RECORDING INNER MENTAL SKILLS ACTIVITY

When you use these skills in your games, make notes on the mental strategies you used. Some issues to note as you pay attention to the good holes and the good shots are:

- Did you follow your pre-shot routine?

- Did you play the shot in a relaxed, confident way?

- Were you committed to the club you chose?

Here is a good way to start. Focus on the positive mental strategies you used in your games. Avoid focusing exclusively on the errors made to learn from your mistakes. When you pay attention to the good shots, you will find that there were many enjoyable moments in the game. This emphasis puts your golf into perspective even if many of your shots do not meet your expectations.

As you become more practiced at this, make the observations more specific. For example:

- What strategies worked well?

- How did you handle distractions?

- Were you able to maintain a good tempo?

- Were you close to your ideal active relaxation level?

- Were some shots played when you were too relaxed, when you were in the relaxation part of your pre-shot routine and not quite ready to make the shot?

Create strategies to get around the problems you came up against. If your visual images are not sharp, you might imagine using a long-lens camera to magnify and sharpen them. If you have a favourite image system, find images in the other systems that appeal to you as well. On some days, I find that visualizing a shot is easier, even though my kinesthetic sense of feeling the swing is my preferred image system. In any case, do not neglect your less favourite image systems – they just might be important in different circumstances, or on a different course.

THE MANZER MODEL DIARY

Len Brayton, a friend of mine, keeps a golf diary by asking himself, "What specific shot made me miss the green in regulation[4] figures?" This is easy for Len, since it means one or two entries per game! Another friend, Carson Manzer is a 16-handicapper who has learnt that forcing himself to ask this same question makes for a better analysis of the hole.

After each game, Carson summarizes the shots that caused him to miss greens in regulation figures. He uses an ordinary course scorecard for the nine categories he requires. But as most cards don't have enough empty rows or columns, he overwrites some of the columns that are meant for other purposes. Figure 3 on page 156 is a scorecard with unlabelled rows and columns, and there is a blank version of it on page 157, for you to photocopy and fold inside the scorecard.

The nine categories to be recorded in the Manzer model, together with his shorthand symbol in brackets to indicate the column (or row), are:

4. Generally, regulation means that you allow yourself two putts a hole. So "regulation" means being on a par 3 green for 1, on a par 5 for 3 and on a par 4 for 2 (Greens In Regulation (GH)).

- Gross score

- Drives (D)

- Fairway woods (FW)

- Full iron shots (I)

- Pitches, less than a full iron shot (P)

- Chips, less than a pitch, and either to the green or out of trouble to the fairway (CH)

- Sand shots from green-side bunkers only (S)

- Putts (these do not require a symbol and are recorded in the handicap row)

- Why? Circle the shot that was responsible for the green not reached in regulation figures

The shorthand symbols used in the recording of shots are:

(#)   a circle around the hole number on the card is a green reached in regulation

✔   a tick for a satisfactory shot

L a shot *Left*, a pull or hook

R a shot *Right*, a push or slice

S a shot *Short* of target

O *Over* the target (instead of long)

WHY ... In the "WHY" column, combine symbols to indicate the shot that caused the missed green. DR is a *Drive* sliced or pushed *Right*.

Here are a few conventions to help simplify record keeping:

- If an iron is used from the tee, record this as an iron shot.

- Fairway bunker shots are fairway shots.

- Write penalty strokes in the same column as putts.

- If you do not hit the ball long, three shots to the green for a long par-four hole may be the figure you have in mind when you ask yourself whether you reached the green in regulation.

ANALYSING THE INFORMATION

Look at Figure 3. For each hole, there is a symbol for each shot, and you add those to the putts to give you your score for that hole. So for hole number 1, there are three ticks and two putts. That's the 5.

Some judgment and interpretation is necessary. For example, on holes 5, one of the two chips shown is because the player had to chip out from trees – and he played it well, as he did the chip on to the green. So while it might look as if he had to chip twice because he messed up the first one, in fact there were two good chips on this hole. Similarly, on hole 14, he drove off the fairway, but he had a good lie and should have made a good fairway wood shot. But this latter shot is the one that prevented him from reaching the green in regulation figures.

A detailed putting record can be added by using the same ideas as in the fairway game, e.g. symbols such as LL for left and long, or PR for pin high but right. An extra row is added to the model form for that.

Figure 3. Model game score card (the blank game card is on page 157, to copy for your own use).

HOLE NO.	①	2	3	4	5	6	⑦	8	9	OUT	10	11	⑫	⑬	14	15	16	⑰	18	IN	PAR	GH: 5
YARDAGE	524	389	373	381	399	307	144	389	188	OUT	374	420	376	149	511	197	300	388	530	IN	PAR	GOOD SHOTS
PAR	5	4	4	4	4	4	3	4	3	35	4	4	4	3	5	3	4	4	5	36	71	
SCORE	5	5	5	5	7	5	2	5	4	43	5	6	4	3	7	5	5	5	5	45	88	
DRIVES	✓	✓	R	✓	R		✓	R	S		✓	S	✓	✓	L	R	✓	✓	✓			9 OF 16
F. WOODS		R		S				S							S		S		S			3 of 8
IRONS	✓		R		R	L					O	L	✓	✓	✓	✓	S	✓	✓			6 of 12
PITCH		✓				O			✓		✓					✓						5 OF 6
CHIPS			✓		✓✓	✓	✓	✓	✓		✓							✓				6 OF 7
SAND SHOTS				S								S										1 OF 3
WHY GREEN MISSED		FR	DR	IR	DR	IL		DR	DS		IO	DS			FS	DR	IS		FS			35 GOOD SHOTS
PUTTS	2	2	2	2	2	2	1	2	2	17	2	2	2	2	3	2	2	3	1	19	36	

Specimen model game score-card for photocopying.

HOLE NO.	1	2	3	4	5	6	7	8	9	10	11	12	13	14	15	16	17	18	GH:
YARDAGE																			
PAR																			
SCORE																			
DRIVES																			
F. WOODS																			
IRONS																			
PITCH																			
CHIPS																			
SAND SHOTS																			
WHY GREEN MISSED																			
PUTTS																			

The following is a natural grouping of the three components of any golf score:

- The fairway game – the sum of the drives, fairway wood shots and iron shots

- The short game – pitches, chips and sand shots

- The putting game.

Carson concerns himself with the number of greens hit in regulation (GH) and with his net field score (NFS.) The NFS is the difference between the gross score and the sum of putts plus penalty strokes (penalty shots add to the gross score but not to the net field score).

Carson has a handicap of 16 and he aims for an NFS of under 50. In this game (Figure 3), his gross score was 88. He used 36 putts, giving him an NFS of 52, which did not meet this goal.

However, he listed 35 of his shots as good shots, a ratio of 35:52, or 70%. His putting game could improve, or perhaps he could be more selective about what he

	Drives	FW	I	Tot	Analysis of the game
Left	0	0	1	1	Of the 13 greens missed: 6 were due to shots to the right, 4 of which were woods. 5 shots were short or topped wood shots. There was no pattern to the missed iron shots.
Right	4	1	1	6	
Short	2	2	1	5	
Over	0	0	1	1	
Totals	6	3	4	13	

Figure 4. Analysis of the game.

considers to be a good chip. He might set a goal of playing his short-game shots to within five feet of the hole, 90% of the time. This would better his putting game because he would have a chance of single-putting more greens.

Figure 4 (above) is the summary of why Carson missed the greens (he is right-handed).

A review of several game summaries, like this example, defines the problems to take to the practice fairway or to your instructor for help. As an example from this one game of Carson's, he wants to correct his tendency to slice or push his shots. This is an intermediate goal toward his performance goal of increasing the number of greens he hits in regulation.

As well as using it to summarize the greens missed, use the card to analyse the game in all categories and record all the ratios. One example in this game is that there were 35 good shots out of the total of 52 shots. Carson also had four good pitch shots out of six tries and six good chips out of seven tries.

The beauty of the method is that it's a very adaptable record that is easy to make, keep and read as it's based on an ordinary score card. So while Carson likes very detailed data keeping, I am less interested in statistical analysis. If you're like me, you can easily modify the method to suit your own needs. For example, I keep a narrative record of my games using the figures gleaned from the card. I always record the number of good shots versus the number of not so good ones, because I tend to remember only the bad ones. In the example card, this is simply recorded as D = 9 of 16 and in your narrative you jot down how many were to the right or left. This provides positive feedback since, as for most golfers, the good outnumbers the not so good.

Neither do I try to tease out which shot prevented me from hitting the green in regulation. I am interested in how close to the hole I get with my chips and pitches. So I don't consider it a good shot if I am fifty feet away from the hole, even though it is on the green and I could count it as a GH.

I use Carson's system as a memory-jogger for my mental strategies, because it is too easy to forget the mental associations of the shots even immediately after a game. I write a narrative diary after a game or a practice session. The model has proved to be very useful to help highlight the shots that I need to analyse and the parts of my game that I should practise.

When we analyze performance, we have to study the errors we made. Beware of the trap of moving from "what is wrong with my game" to "there is something wrong with me". As with good shots, learn from the not-so-good ones. Never, ever think of them as failures. It is too easy to generalize with such a powerful word, to think of yourself as a failure because you have made an error.

Do take the next step and work on the lessons learned from analyzing your games. Otherwise, the effort is wasted and this may turn you against keeping records of your games before seeing the benefits of a diary.

IS ALL THIS NEW?
THEORETICAL
CONSIDERATIONS

LEFT AND RIGHT BRAIN

Athletes commonly say "the less you think, the better you perform", because you use your sequentially analytical left-brain less and your intuitively creative right brain more. Golfers have to avoid "paralysis by analysis" in their pre-shot routine. With practice, you will learn to trust your right-brain functions and balance them with your left-brain activities. The best human performances occur when the functions of both sides of the brain are integrated and coordinated. For example, electroencephalogram (EEG) studies of a concert violinist showed that both sides of his brain were very active during a performance. The brain activity of his audience was mainly on the right side.

Studies of right- and left-brain function form the theoretical background for this program. Left-brain activity is the dominant mode in our everyday work. We analyse and use sequential logic to solve problems. When we hit a block, we switch to right-brain activity. For example, we "sleep on the problem", or just take a break. The right brain is more involved with creativity, nonverbal understanding, kinaesthetic and spatial images and modelling. Feel, touch and tempo are also located here.

However, the brain is a very complicated organ indeed and we can't define a neat left and right division. Many functions and activities are represented on both sides of the brain. Right-brain involvement shows up on the EEG, so we can see increased right-brain activity during the altered states of hypnosis and meditation. (See Figure 1 on page 80.)

ULTRADIAN RHYTHMS

We are all familiar with the faraway look of students during a lecture, or someone staring into space for a few minutes during their work. Dr Milton Erickson, a prominent modern psychotherapist, also noticed that most people slip into a sort of trance fairly often throughout the day. He called these episodes "common everyday trances" and incorporated them into his therapy sessions.

Dr Ernest Rossi also studied the idea and had his patients record their daily activities in detail. He confirmed that we have a *basic rest–activity cycle* (BRAC), which has a period ranging from 90 to 120 minutes. As we daydream, we shift to right-brain dominance. It seems that the brain needs a rest from its usual control activity and shifts body systems into their maintenance mode for a time. This maintenance mode is marked by an increase in intestinal and urinary activity. There are respiratory changes indicated by a yawn or a sigh. The heart rate slows and the skin warms. It is "take-a-break" time, when you get up and move around, go to the bathroom, have a drink or do something to feel relaxed. Most of us are not aware of these cycles and, if there is much stimulation in our environment, it is easy to ignore the signals. Researchers call these daydreaming cycles *ultradian rhythms*, which means they last less than a day. We are more aware of the sleep–wake cycle, which lasts about a day and is called a *circadian* (Latin for "about") cycle. Researchers have found many circadian cycles in our hormonal production, like cortisols, which peak in the late afternoon and are at their lowest level in the early morning.

Being aware of ultradian rhythms will allow you to recognize the rest-period part of your day. This may be the best stress reliever you have. Take a small portion of the rest period to direct your daydreams about your golf game. This will not interfere with the natural benefit of the rejuvenation period, but it will certainly add to your practice time for such things as reviewing your pre-shot routine or practicing anchors in your imagination.

RELAXATION

Remember, the relaxation that golfers strive for in their shot making is not the deep level found in TM, hypnosis or other techniques used in therapy. Rather, it is an active relaxation in which the muscles that oppose an active muscle have just the right amount of tone to allow that active muscle to function at its best. Leif Janson found that his best archers had this ability in spades. The best athletes in every sport he studied had the same capability, as did the best stringed-instrument players. So it follows that all performers require the ability to establish active relaxation, meaning they require just the right tone in opposing muscles to perform well.

During the 1994 Swedish Master's tournament, Janson took the opportunity to study golfers with different levels of ability. The tracing and graphics of the muscle activity of the extensor muscles of the right forearms of two players are presented in Figures 5 and 5a. The ability of the better golfer to perform with a smooth controlled

Ian Woosnam

EMG test i samband med
scandinavian masters 1994~07~26

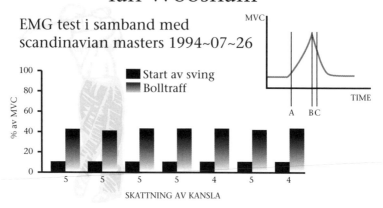

Figure 5.

Golfare strax under
elitnivå

EMG test 1994~07~26

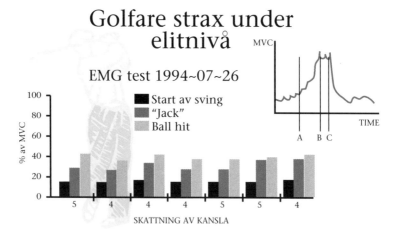

Figure 5a.

Figure 5 shows a graph of seven shots by Ian Woosnam. The bars show the muscle activity of his extensor muscles during his swings. The right-hand bar is his grip pressure at the start, the second bar is at ball strike. Grip pressure is measured as a percentage of the maximum voluntary contraction (MVC) of these muscles. The inset is the electromyographic (EMG) tracing of one swing. There is no unnecessary muscle activity in his takeaway nor in his downswing, so there are only two bars shown. The numbers below the bars indicate his estimate of the outcome of the shots, 5 being the best. Janson found Woosnam's swing to be the smoothest and most accurate he tested.

Figure 5a depicts the graph of a less skilled player. The middle bar shows the "unwished-for" muscle activity during his takeaway and at the top of his back swing. The EMG tracing indicates this extra activity throughout his swing. (Janson calls this "Jack" in the graph.) Notice the variability of the grip pressure throughout his swing. This player accepts this extra muscle activity as a normal part of his swing, judging from his assessment of the outcome of each shot. Janson found that some good players have 100% of their MVC at the top of the back swing and at ball strike and are unaware of this because they are so used to their technique.

(The graphs in these figures are reprinted with permission of Leif Janson from his studies made at the Swedish Masters tournament, July 26, 1994. He published them in his book *Avspänd Teknik*.)

muscle action is well illustrated in the actual tracings inset in the diagrams. The graphs represent seven swings of each player. Notice how the better player uses the same force for each swing. In contrast, notice the variability of muscle activity in the player of lesser ability. Notice also that he was satisfied with shots that were made with much unnecessary activity in his opposing muscles.

Janson also found that good golfers are so used to their own technique that they cannot feel, or do not know, what happens in their swing. For example, he reported that some of these good players had nearly 100% of their maximum voluntary isometric contraction (MVC)[5] at the top of their back swing. They gripped the club very hard at this point in their swing. Other players did this at the point of ball-strike. Both habits would tend to produce errant shots. Janson used biofeedback to teach these players to smooth out this unnecessary muscle activity with excellent results. The tour players concerned were gratified with the results, too!

Can this skill be taught? For a professional athlete looking for the edge he needs to win, biofeedback

5. Maximum Voluntary Contraction (MVC) is a term in kinesiology. The subject is asked to grip as hard as possible to get a base line figure for comparison within that individual, in this case grip pressure. It is usually measured indirectly by electromyographic (EMG) means, as this allows for measurements during performance as in Leif Janson's study.

technology would be cost-effective. Swedish researchers used the well-known PMR, or progressive muscle relaxation, because it is always available to athletes and is the best method for basic training in this skill. They found that it took an adult four weeks of twice-daily sessions of PMR to learn the correct level of relaxation in those muscle groups important to their sport. Dedicated athletes were highly motivated, putting in twenty-minute sessions twice daily until they mastered this muscle control.

Results of this simple exercise are impressive. I can vouch for its effectiveness in my golf game and in my skiing. I put in a month of daily PMR sessions before the skiing season and I believe I am skiing with more relaxed, controlled turns than ever before. Moreover, I no longer have the painful calf muscle that used to plague me for several days after a day's skiing. I believe my calf muscles are relaxed because I no longer try to hold on to my boot with my toes during turns.

HISTORICAL CONSIDERATIONS

The phenomenon of the altered state has always been a part of human existence. The ancients incorporated it into their prayer rituals and healing practices. This can now be found in cultures comparatively untouched by civilization. In eighteenth-century Europe there was a strong belief in possession by good and bad spirits, with the bad spirits causing illness. Alongside it sat a strong tradition of faith healing, with many physicians and priests involved in its use.

MESMERISM

An Austrian physician named Franz Anton Mesmer (1734–1815) showed that he could cure patients using his method just as well as a famous faith healer who claimed miracle cures using the exorcism rite.

Mesmer lived at the beginning of the Age of Enlightenment, when people thought that science would eventually explain all of the phenomena of the natural world. Magnetism had been discovered and Mesmer theorized that his technique tapped into this force to cure illness. He called this use of magnetism *animal magnetism*, the first cohesive theory to explain the phenomenon in what we now call hypnosis.

In Mesmer's clinics, the patients held on to metal rods placed in water containing iron filings. He would appear in flowing purple robes and make passes over the patients with his hands. After the magnetic show, he would talk with his patients (perhaps the first psychotherapist). Some cures did occur and Mesmer and his followers soon became popular, despite vigorous opposition from the conservative Medical Faculty in Paris. The Royal Society of Science set up a Commission of Inquiry headed by Benjamin Franklin, who was then American ambassador to France. The inquiry disproved the theory of animal magnetism but did not dispute the cures, saying only that the cures were due to the influence of the patient's imagination. Mesmer became disenchanted with the Medical Faculty's stubbornness in refusing even to consider his theories, and never achieved his dream of being accepted by his physician peers. He left Paris and retired from medicine.

FROM MESMERISM TO HYPNOSIS

Physicians across Europe continued to use the technique because it could be used for pain relief during surgery. James Esdaile (1808–68), a surgeon working with the East India Company, reported using mesmerism as the only anaesthetic in more than a thousand surgical operations – 350 of which were major procedures. Not only were the operations successful, but also both the morbidity rate (infections and blood loss) and the mortality rate were less than half those expected, despite the primitive conditions. He continued this practice with equal success when he returned to Britain. When ether and then chloroform became available in the 1840s, interest in mesmerism for surgical anaesthesia declined.

Physicians of that time were puzzled by patients who were deeply mesmerized and seemingly without pain during surgical procedures. James Braid (1795–1860), an eye surgeon in Scotland, theorized that it was related to sleep and coined the word *hypnosis*, feeling that it was a type of nervous sleep (the word comes from *hypnos*, the Greek word for sleep). He introduced the technique in which the patient focused on a watch waving like a pendulum to enter the mesmeric state.

Later in the century, Jean Martin Charcot (1825–93), a leading neurologist in Paris, linked hypnosis to hysteria, a disease state. Although this theory about hypnosis was more acceptable to the scientific community, it was soon discarded. He was working with institutionalized mental patients, not a representative cross-section of people. Some of these patients may have had hysterical symptoms and many had a self-interest in obeying Dr Charcot, since he was also head of the hospital.

A country doctor named August Ambrose Liébault (1823–1904) and a neurologist from the city of Nancy, Hippolyte Bernheim (1840–1919), developed the theory, unlike Charcot's, that hypnosis was connected to a person's suggestibility. A colleague, Emile Coué (1856–1926), astutely observed that, to be effective, an instruction had to become a self-suggestion. These three practitioners dealt with the general population and well recognized the variability in their patients' capability to use these mental skills. Coué is responsible for the generic self-suggestion, "Every day in every way, I am better and better." Affirmations, like those in this program, are based on this idea.

MODERN IDEAS

In World War II, psychiatrists used hypnosis to treat battle fatigue because they saw a link between the mental state of soldiers and the dissociation theory of Dr Pierre Janet (1859–1947), Charcot's successor in Paris. (Dissociation means that we have the ability to be in two or more places at once through our imaging capability. Danny Kaye's *Walter Mitty* is an excellent comedy on this theme.)

Dentists used hypnosis for pain control when local anaesthetic supplies ran out during that war. Since then, there has been a surge of interest and research in hypnosis, particularly relating to the mind–body connection.

How does the mind affect the immune system? Dr Karen Olness, a paediatric immunologist, has shown that children can increase the immune protein material (some of these proteins are antibodies) in their saliva. In her experiment, three groups of children were shown a movie of how the immune system works. The first control group saw only the movie. The second control group were asked to think about what they had seen in the movie. The third group of children, the experimental group, were asked to "direct their dreams" by creating images of increasing amounts of immune protein in their saliva. They did so to levels well above the two control groups. Dr Olness called this ability *cyberphysiologic control* (*cyber* comes from the Greek *kybernetes*, meaning to steer.) She reported (at the *"Frontiers of Hypnosis"* an international conference in Banff, Alberta, Canada, in May 1995) that a follow-up study in Australia proved the effectiveness of this strategy. Schoolchildren, taught how to increase immune proteins in their saliva, had a much lower incidence of respiratory infections during the "colds season", shown by fewer absences from school.

Dr Lars Eric Unestähl, whom we met earlier, noticed that the behaviour and attitudes that athletes develop during a peak performance are also well developed in patients who cope best with serious illness. He called this behaviour the "ideal health state". One implication of this observation is that everyone can learn these skills. This implies that the inner mental skills we associate with sport can enhance health, improve education, help with business success and be applied to the workplace. In Sweden, the spread of mental training into other fields is already well advanced. For example, Swedish police find the training helpful in managing the potentially difficult situations they encounter.

PERSUASION AND THE PLACEBO EFFECT

A brief explanation of how and why we pay attention to a stimulus from our surroundings may help clarify this process. It is one explanation of the process of concentration. After a stimulus hits the sense organ, a signal is generated and proceeds through the brain, where it interacts with memories and their associated feelings. These modify the image created by the stimulus. It is the strength of the signal when it reaches the cerebral cortex, and therefore your awareness, that decides the attention you give it. This awareness includes the feelings associated with the images. A person who has a phobia to snakes has a rush of fearful feelings at the sight of a snake, so he pays a great deal of attention to that snake!

Feedback from a memory of a previous experience can increase the strength of the signal if the associated emotions are there. If you focus on the negative images – "I've missed short putts like this one before" – then you cannot concentrate on the positive image of making the putt. Practicing the positive imagery related to putting – such as, "I've made hundreds of putts like this one" – will reinforce your confidence and so your ability to concentrate on that putt. A shot out of sand may be unnecessarily difficult if your image of this shot is one of driving the club through the sand with great effort. You will tend to focus on the effort and likely spoil the shot. Changing this image to one where the club head slides through the sand under the ball with little effort on its way to the finish of the swing produces a positive change in both attitude and performance.

Once we learn to reprogram the "software" in our brains like this, we can use this skill in positive ways. We can persuade ourselves to be more positive in performance. We can persuade ourselves to increase the antibodies in our saliva to combat the infectious agents that most often enter through the mouth. We can also persuade ourselves to modify our perception of pain, a useful skill even with modern medical technology.

A surgeon friend with a peptic ulcer noticed that, when he woke at night with ulcer pain, the pain would often disappear before he took his antacid. The expectation of pain relief was as important as the antacid. This phenomenon is called the *placebo effect*, usually described as the same effect produced with a sugar pill as with the real thing. I believe that when you use your inner mental skills, you tap into this complex placebo phenomenon. We all experience the placebo effect. Up to 60% of the effect of any (genuine) pill can be the result of the placebo effect. Researchers go to great lengths to determine how much of the effect of a new medication is due to this effect.

George Peper, in his lead editorial of the August 1996 *Golf Magazine*, discusses "the 45-day rule". This rule states that you can have a 45-day honeymoon with a new golf club, but the magic will not last for ever because of the placebo effect. That is, you hit the ball longer because you believe the club is better, just as you believe the sugar pill is the real thing. The 45-day rule can be broken. The placebo effect can last as long as you want it to when you use your inner mental skills and learn to trust yourself to play well.

A complete explanation of what happens during the hypnotic or meditative state is not yet available. An interesting newer idea is that it belongs with the art of persuasion. The literature on this includes that of sales ability and the art of rhetoric. Alan Scheflin, a lawyer who studies hypnosis from his legal background, spoke of this idea in Banff Albeta, at the 1995 conference, *"Frontiers of Hypnosis"*.

When you use self-suggestion, you are using a form of persuasion. When you make suggestions that evoke images such as seeing and feeling yourself achieving your goals, you are using your total mind. This is a very powerful, positive and persuasive force for good in your life as well as in your golf game.

Another new idea that may have implications for the problem of transferring good shots from the practice range to the course has appeared in *The Sports Psychologist* (2003), Volume 16, pp. 79–99. It is entitled "Rapid Technique Correction Using Old Way/New Way: Two Case Studies With Olympic Athletes" (Yuri Hanen, Tapio Kojus, Petteri Jouste, Paul Baxter). The authors report on a preliminary study, part of a much larger multidisciplinary project funded by the Finnish Ministry of Education, which uses a method developed for children with spelling difficulties. The basic premise of the method is that athletes in the stress of a competition revert to an "old" technique learned earlier by themselves, even though they use the "new" correct technique very well in practice. For children, the terms "wrong way" and "right way", which are usually used in the classroom, carry too much emotional charge when used by an authority figure, e.g. a teacher. Do not forget, we all carry our child from the past inside our unconscious minds, so adults, too, may find the terms "old way" and "new way" easier to accept.

The method involves writing the old spelling of the word, (for example *sed*) then the new spelling (*said*) opposite on the same line. This is done five times. Then the new spelling is written ten times with the last five using the new spelling in a sentence each time (I said; my mom said to my sister; my dad said to me; etc.).

The example in athletics was a javelin thrower who lowered her arm to hip level in competition and lost considerable distance, well below Olympic standards. She knew she could throw well and so was reluctant to do the experiment because she knew the proper way. So her coach persuaded her to give it a try using a video of her throws in competition. She followed the method, reinforced by repeating her two types of throws with her eyes closed. They also videotaped the exercises. As part of the study, the authors found that the new way reverted to the old way in two weeks, but that the athlete knew how to get around the problem by herself.

I am intrigued with the ideas involved and have used them to teach a golfer to change his putting stroke from a stroke that stopped at the ball, a jab, to a smooth stroke through the ball to the hole. That was a very simple problem, but the swing is a very complicated movement and it is difficult to tease out one thing that gets us into trouble in the problem of practice range versus course play. To be successful, the cooperation of a perceptive coach with video help to work together with a mental trainer very familiar with the ideas would be a necessity. The authors give an example of a coach who knew of the method and tried it, but failed because he did not fully understand the method, so do not try it yourself unless you have the professional background to learn it well and a cooperative coach to help you. Nevertheless, a very intriguing study.

The authors have a grant to pursue their ideas and are studying professional golfers, alpine skiers, and swimmers as well as the track and field athletes, but I have not seen a new report as yet.

BIBLIOGRAPHY AND RESOURCES

Benson, Herbert (1984), *Beyond the Relaxation Response* (New York, NY: Times Books). An excellent book, and a good introduction to the ideas of this program.

Botterill Lifestyles (1986), *Visualization: What You See Is What You Get* (videotape) (Coaching Association of Canada). An excellent presentation for coaches on visualization in a variety of sports. Golf is not mentioned, because they focus on Olympic athletes.

Cohn, Patrick J. (1991), "An Exploratory Study on Peak Performance in Golf", *Sport Psychologist*, 5: 5–14. One of many such studies into this fascinating aspect of human performance experience.

Enhager, Kjell, and Samantha Wallace (1991), *Quantum Golf* (New York, NY: Warner Books). Written in the manner of *Golf in the Kingdom*, but from the perspective of the quantum theories of Depak Chopra.

Grinder, John, and Richard Bandler (1981), *Trance-formations* (Moab, UT: Real People Press). This and several other books by these authors are the original introduction to neuro-linguistic programming (NLP). The second problem-solving exercise in this book is an example of one such technique.

Hall, E. G., and C. J. Hardy (1981), "Using the Right Brain in Sport", in J. Salmella, J. Parkington and T. Orlick (eds), *New Paths to Sport Learning* (Ottawa: Coaching Association of Canada). This article surveys the theory as applied to sport. There are several good articles in this manual, including an early one by Uneståhl.

Haultain, Arnold (1908), *The Mystery of Golf* (Cambridge, MA/Boston, MA: Applewood Books). Reprinted in 1965 and 1986 with a Foreword by Herbert Warren Wind, in which he says: "It may very well be, as some of its admirers have claimed, the equivalent among books on golf to what Izaak Walton's *The Compleat Angler* is to fishing."

Hogan, Charles (1988), *Nice Shot*, (videotape and booklet) (Columbia, SC: Sports Enhancement Associates).

Jensen, Peter (1993), *Golfer's Inside Edge* (audiotape presentation) (Rockwood, ON: Performance Coaching Inc.).

Loehr, James E. (1994), *The New Toughness Training for Sports* (New York, NY: Penguin Books USA). The author's extensive experience with high-performance athletes, including tour players, provides the basis of programming yourself for competition. His daily diary model is very comprehensive.

Mackenzie, Marlin M. (1990), *Golf: The Mind Game* (New York, NY: Dell Publishing). A master practitioner of neuro-linguistic programming, he outlines many NLP techniques for solving golf problems.

Miller, John (1990), "One-Day Wonders", *Golf Illustrated*, October. He talks about "the little voice that talks to me". This is very reminiscent of the inner coach that I talk of in this program.

Murphy, Michael (1972), *Golf in the Kingdom* (New York, NY: Viking Press). This classic has been recently re-released. A must book for the serious and the not so serious golfer interested in the mind and human performance. He speaks through the mythical Scottish pro, Shivas Irons.

Olness K., T. Culbert and D. Uden (1989), "Self-Regulation of Salivary Immunoglobulin A by Children", *Pediatrics*, Vol. 83, No. 1, January. An excellent article on the ability of the mind to affect the immune system.

Orlick, Terry (1986), *Psyching for Sport* (Champaign, IL: Leisure Press). Organizer of the 1995 World Congress on Mental Training and Excellence in Ottawa, he is an internationally renowned writer and speaker on mental preparation for sport. His work with Olympic athletes is the subject of this book.

Peper, George (1996), "Tee Dance" *Golf Magazine*, August. This editorial discusses the placebo effect associated with owning a new club that works well for you: the 45-day rule. It works because the player believes that it is better. The effect lasts about six weeks.

Price, Charles (1984), "What is a Player?", *Golf Digest*, April. A description of a person who plays the game of golf versus one who is a golfer. Perhaps we should all aspire to the description of a player that Price writes about.

Pulos, Lee (1990), *Beyond Hypnosis* (San Francisco and Vancouver: Omega Press). He has a long experience consulting with professional hockey and football players as well as Olympians. He has also studied healing practices in cultures untouched by Western ideas. He blends the practical with the theoretical to point toward the "Future Mind", his view of the potential of the human mind in all aspects of life.

Rossi, Ernest L. (1991), *The Twenty-Minute Break: the Ultradian Healing Response* (Los Angeles, CA: Jeremy Tarcher). A practical guide to the basic rest–activity cycle and its everyday applications.

Rotella, Bob, and Bob Cullen (1995), *Golf is Not a Game of Perfect* (New York, NY: Simon & Schuster). An excellent book written in a conversational manner with anecdotes and experiences from tour players on mental preparation for golf. He has a straightforward approach to attitudes and behaviours for playing better golf.

Rubenstein, Lorne (1996), "Different Strokes", *Senior Golfer*, August, pp. 42–9. He has written many articles on Moe Norman. This one includes "Moe's Musings", pithy sayings from Moe. The quotation at the top of Chapter Five is from this article.

Scheflin, Alan W. (1995), "The Current Assaults on Hypnosis and Therapy", presentation at "Frontiers of Hypnosis" conference, Banff, Alberta, Canada, in May in which he talked about the art of persuasion.

Tribble, Curt, and Doug Newberg (1995), "Dealing with Sub-optimal Outcomes", presentation at "Mental Training and Excellence" conference, Ottawa, May. I learned the idea of forgiving oneself for errors from their talk on performance education in graduate medical education.

Unestähl, Lars Eric (ed.) (1986), "Contemporary Sport Psychology", proceedings of the VI World Congress in Sport Psychology, Örebro, Sweden (Veje Publishing Inc., Örebro, Sweden). Dr Unestähl is a world-renowned authority on mental training. He is a founding faculty member of the Scandinavian International University in Örebro, Sweden, and is president of the International Society for Mental Training. The second world congress of the society was held in Ottawa in May 1995.

Unestähl, Lars Eric (1989), "Mental Skills for Sport and Life", paper given at the VII World Congress in Sport Psychology, Singapore, August 1989. (This paper outlines the Swedish experience with Inner Mental Training and the research background for the programs. This and other pamphlets are available from Dr Uneståhl at The Scandinavian International University, P.O. Box 3085, S-70003, Örebro, Sweden.)

Uneståhl, Lars Eric, and Pavel Bundsen (1996) "Neuro-Biochemical Mechanisms and Psycho-Physical Consequences", *Hypnos*, Vol. XXIII, No. 3, pp. 148–56. A Swedish/Russian study of EEG tracings during mental training. Athletes, students of all ages and health workers were studied.

Williams, Jean M. (ed.) (1986), *Applied Sport Psychology* (Palo Alto, CA: Mayfield Publishing Company). Robert M. Nideffer, an expert on concentration in sport, has an excellent chapter in this book. Ken Ravizza's chapter on peak performance is also good. Uneståhl has a chapter on his early experience on hypnosis in sport.

INDEX

ABOUT THE AUTHOR

Tom Saunders MD, has merged his life's work as a physician with his life's pleasure, golf. As a doctor, he enjoyed
many years teaching self-hypnosis to patients. As a
professor, he taught medical students and trainees in

family medicine how to use the techniques to help their patients manage medical problems. Noticing the similarity between self-hypnosis and mental training programs for Olympians led him to try the techniques for his own game. When he improved, he taught the techniques to golfers and other athletes, helping them reach their potential. This experience became the basis of this program, *Golf: Lower Your Score With Mental Training*.

A professor emeritus at the University of Calgary, Dr Saunders is a graduate of McGill University with an MA in medical education from Michigan State University. He plays to a 12 handicap.

Dr Saunders can be contacted at:

Phone: (403) 240-3036
Email: mbgmd@telusplanet.net
105 Sierra Morena Terrace SW
Calgary, Alberta, Canada T3H 3A2